THIS IS
MARKETING

THIS IS MARKETING

Seth Godin

PORTFOLIO / PENGUIN

Portfolio/Penguin
An imprint of Penguin Random House LLC
375 Hudson Street
New York, New York 10014

Most Portfolio books are available at a discount when purchased in quantity for sales promotions or corporate use. Special editions, which include personalized covers, excerpts, and corporate imprints, can be created when purchased in large quantities. For more information, please call (212) 572–2232 or email specialmarkets@penguinrandomhouse.com. Your local bookstore can also assist with discounted bulk purchases using the Penguin Random House corporate Business-to-Business program. For assistance in locating a participating retailer, email B2B@penguinrandomhouse.com.

Library of Congress Cataloging-in-Publication Data

Names: Godin, Seth, author.
Title: This is marketing / Seth Godin.
Description: New York : Portfolio/Penguin, [2018] | Includes index.
Identifiers: LCCN 2018041567 (print) | LCCN 2018042423 (ebook) |
ISBN 9780525540847 (Ebook) | ISBN 9780525540830 (hardcover)
Subjects: LCSH: Marketing.
Classification: LCC HF5415 (ebook) | LCC HF5415 .G5783 2018 (print) |
DDC 658.8--dc23
LC record available at https://lccn.loc.gov/2018041567

Printed in the United States of America
10 9 8 7 6 5 4 3 2 1

BOOK DESIGN BY LUCIA BERNARD

N DOLLARS AND IMPACTED MORE THAN SEVEN
CARROT DELIVERED MORE THAN 400,000
NG (AND CHANGES CORPORATIONS) SELLING
MICHELLE KYDD LEE CO-FOUNDED A GROUP
REAT FARM WORKERS AS WELL. GLOWFORGE
F LASER CUTTERS. MICHAEL FEELEY, A REAL
FOUND THE RIGHT PEOPLE FOR THE RIGHT
TA ISIBO AND MUHIRE PATRICK BOTH MAKE
R BRANDS IN THE U.S. AND AROUND THE
PROTECTS THE PRIVACY OF ITS USERS, SETS
HAS SOLD MORE THAN 2,000 PAINTINGS.
VILLAGES THAT HAD NONE. SCOTT PERRY
HIS CLIENTS, NONE OF WHOM HE'D MET
SENBERG BUILT CREATIVE MORNINGS INTO A
0 CITIES. SHAWN ASKINOSIE CHANGED THE
PAYING THEM TRIPLE THE PREVAILING WAGE.
OF RESTAURANTS AND CHANGED THE WAY
NGAY STANIER SOLD 150,000 COPIES OF
ANDA PALMER MADE ART FOR HER 11,000
0 ALUMNI WHO ARE MAKING A RUCKUS . . .

For Leo, Anna, Mo, Sammy, Alex, Bernadette, and Shawn . . .
And for all the fresh voices that make our lives better

CONTENTS

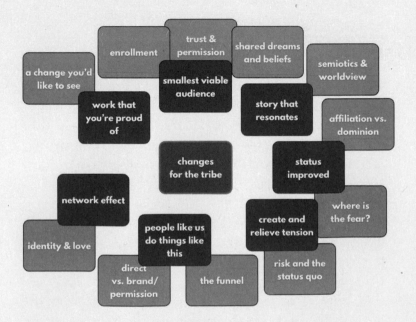

[a sketch to show you what's to come]

Marketing is all around us. From your very first memories to the moment before you opened this book, you've been inundated by marketing. You learned to read from the logos on the side of the road, and you spend your time and your money in response to what marketers have paid to put in front of you. Marketing, more than a lake or a forest, is the landscape of our modern lives.

Because marketing has been done to us for so long, we take it for granted. Like the fish who doesn't understand water, we fail to see what's actually happening, and don't notice how it's changing us.

It's time to do something else with marketing. To make things better. To cause a change you'd like to see in the world. To grow your project, sure, but mostly to serve the people you care about.

The answer to just about every question about work is really the question, "Who can you help?"

This is marketing

- Marketing seeks *more*. More market share, more customers, more work.
- Marketing is driven by better. Better service, better community, better outcomes.
- Marketing creates culture. Status, affiliation, and people like us.
- Most of all, marketing is change.
- Change the culture, change your world.
- Marketers make change happen.
- Each of us is a marketer, and each of us has the ability to make more change than we imagined. Our opportunity and our obligation is to do marketing that we're proud of.

How tall is your sunflower?

That's what most people seem to care about. How big a brand, how much market share, how many online followers. Too many marketers spend most of their time running a hype show, trying to get just a little bigger.

The thing is, tall sunflowers have deep and complex root systems. Without them, they'd never get very high.

This is a book about roots. About anchoring your work deeply in the dreams, desires, and communities of those you seek to serve. It's about changing people for the better, creating work you can be proud of. And it's about being a driver of the market, not simply being market-driven.

We can do work that matters for people who care. If you're like most of my readers, I don't think you'd have it any other way.

It's not going to market itself

The best ideas aren't instantly embraced. Even the ice cream sundae and the stoplight took years to catch on.

That's because the best ideas require significant change. They fly in the face of the status quo, and inertia is a powerful force.

Because there's a lot of noise and a lot of distrust. Change is risky.

And because we often want others to go first.

Your most generous and insightful work needs help finding the people it's meant to serve. And your most successful work will spread because you designed it to.

Marketing isn't just selling soap

When you give a TED Talk, you're marketing.

When you ask your boss for a raise, you're marketing.

When you raise money for the local playground, you're marketing.

And yes, when you're trying to grow your division at work, that's marketing too.

For a long time, during the days when marketing and advertising were the same thing, marketing was reserved for vice presidents with a budget.

And now it's for you.

The market decides

You've built something amazing. You have a living to make. Your boss wants more sales. That nonprofit you care about, an important one, needs to raise money. Your candidate is polling poorly. You want the boss to approve your project . . .

Why isn't it working? If creating is the point, if writing and painting and building are so fun, why do we even care if we're found, recognized, published, broadcast, or otherwise commercialized?

Marketing is the act of making change happen. Making is insufficient. You haven't made an impact until you've changed someone.

Changed the boss's mind.

Changed the school system.

Changed demand for your product.

You can do this by creating and then relieving tension. By establishing cultural norms. By seeing status roles and helping to change them (or maintain them).

But first, you need to see it. Then you need to choose to work with human beings to help them find what they're looking for.

How to know if you have a marketing problem

You aren't busy enough.

Your ideas aren't spreading.

The community around you isn't what it could be.

The people you care about aren't achieving everything they hoped.

Your politician needs more votes, your work isn't fulfilling, your customers are frustrated . . .

If you see a way to make things better, you now have a marketing problem.

The answer to a movie

Filmmaker and showrunner Brian Koppelman uses the expression "the answer to a movie," as if a movie is a problem.

But, of course, it is. It's the problem of unlocking the viewer (or the producer, or the actor, or the director). To gain enrollment. To have them let you in. To get a chance to tell your story, and then, even better, to have that story make an impact.

Just as a movie is a problem, so is the story of your marketing. It has to resonate with the listener, to tell them something they've been waiting to hear, something they're open to believing. It has to invite them on a journey where a change might happen. And then, if you've opened all those doors, it has to solve the problem, to deliver on the promise.

You have a marketing question, and it's possible that there's an answer.

But only if you look for it.

Marketing your work is a complaint on the way to better

They say that the best way to complain is to make things better.

It's difficult to do that if you can't spread the word, can't share those ideas, or can't get paid for the work you do.

The first step on the path to make things better is to make better things.

But better isn't only up to you. Better can't happen in a vacuum.

Better is the change we see when the market embraces what we're offering. Better is what happens when the culture absorbs our work and improves. Better is when we make the dreams of those we serve come true.

Marketers make things better by making change happen.

Sharing your path to better is called marketing, and you can do it. We all can.

For more on the ideas in this book, please visit
www.TheMarketingSeminar.com

CHAPTER ONE

Not Mass, Not Spam, Not Shameful . . .

Marketing has changed, but our understanding of what we're supposed to do next hasn't kept up. When in doubt, we selfishly shout. When in a corner, we play small ball, stealing from our competition instead of broadening the market. When pressed, we assume that everyone is just like us, but uninformed.

Mostly, we remember growing up in a mass market world, where TV and the Top 40 hits defined us. As marketers, we seek to repeat the old-fashioned tricks that don't work anymore.

The compass points toward trust

Every three hundred thousand years or so, the north pole and the south pole switch places. The magnetic fields of the Earth flip.

In our culture, it happens more often than that.

And in the world of culture change, it just happened. The true north, the method that works best, has flipped. Instead of selfish mass, effective marketing now relies on empathy and service.

In this book, we're working together to solve a set of related problems. How to spread your ideas. How to make the impact you seek. How to improve the culture.

There isn't an obvious road map. No simple step-by-step series of tactics. But what I can promise you is a compass: a true north. A recursive method that will get better the more you use it.

This book is based on a hundred-day seminar, one that involves not just lessons but peer-to-peer coaching around shared work. In TheMarketingSeminar.com we assemble thousands of marketers and challenge them to go deeper, to share their journey, to challenge each other to see what truly works.

As you read through, don't hesitate to backtrack, to redo an assumption, to question an existing practice—you can adjust, test, measure, and repeat.

Marketing is one of our greatest callings. It's the work of positive change. I'm thrilled that you're on this journey, and I hope you'll find the tools you need here.

Marketing is not a battle, and it's not a war, or even a contest

Marketing is the generous act of helping someone solve a problem. Their problem.

It's a chance to change the culture for the better.

Marketing involves very little in the way of shouting, hustling, or coercion.

It's a chance to serve, instead.

The internet is the first mass medium that wasn't invented to make marketers happy. Television was invented to hold TV ads, and radio was invented to give radio ads a place to live.

But the internet isn't built around interruption and mass. It's the largest medium, but it's also the smallest one. There's no mass, and you can't steal attention for a penny the way your grandparents' companies did. To be really clear: the internet feels like a vast, free media playground, a place where all your ideas deserve to be seen by just about everyone. In fact, it's a billion tiny whispers, an endless series of selfish conversations that rarely include you or the work you do.

The magic of ads is a trap that keeps us from building a useful story

For a long time, the most efficient way for a commercial enterprise to make large-scale change was simple: buy ads. Ads worked. Ads were a bargain. Ads paid for themselves. Besides, they were fun to make. You could buy a lot all at once. They made you (or your brand) a little famous. And they were reliable: money spent equaled sales made.

Is it any wonder that, pretty quickly, marketers decided that advertising was what they did? For most of my lifetime, marketing *was* advertising.

And then it wasn't true anymore.

Which means you'll need to become a marketer instead.

That means seeing what others see. Building tension. Aligning with tribes. Creating ideas that spread. It means doing the hard work of becoming driven by the market and working with (your part of) that market.

On getting the word out (precisely the wrong question)

"How do I get the word out?"

The SEO expert promises that you will be found when people search for you.

The Facebook consultant tells you how to interrupt just the right people.

The PR professional promises articles and mentions and profiles.

And Don Draper, David Ogilvy, and the rest will trade your money for ads. Beautiful, sexy, effective ads.

All to get the word out.

But that's not marketing, not anymore. And it doesn't work, not anymore.

We're going to talk about how you'll be discovered. *But it's the last part, not the first.*

Marketing is important enough to do right, which means doing the other part first.

Shameless marketers brought shame to the rest of us

A short-term, profit-maximizing hustler can easily adopt a shameless mind-set. Spamming, tricking, coercing. Is there any other profession that proudly does this?

You won't find civil engineers who call senior citizens in the middle of the night to sell them worthless collectible coins. You won't hear of accountants who extract customers' data without permission, or orchestra conductors who proudly post fake reviews online.

This shameless pursuit of attention at the expense of the truth has driven many ethical and generous marketers to hide their best work, to feel shame about the prospect of being market-driven.

That's not okay.

The other kind of marketing, the effective kind, is about understanding our customers' worldview and desires so we can connect with them. It's focused on being missed when you're gone, on bringing more than people expect to those who trust us. It seeks volunteers, not victims.

There's a groundswell of people doing marketing because they know they can make things better. They're prepared to engage with the market because they know they can contribute to our culture.

People like you.

The lock and the key

It doesn't make any sense to make a key and then run around looking for a lock to open.

The only productive solution is to find a lock and then fashion a key.

It's easier to make products and services for the customers you seek to serve than it is to find customers for your products and services.

Marketing doesn't have to be selfish

In fact, the best marketing never is.

Marketing is the generous act of helping others become who they seek to become. It involves creating honest stories—stories that resonate and spread. Marketers offer solutions, opportunities for humans to solve their problems and move forward.

And when our ideas spread, we change the culture. We build something that people would miss if it were gone, something that gives them meaning, connection, and possibility.

The other kind of marketing—the hype, scams, and pressure—thrives on selfishness. I know that it doesn't work in the long run, and that you can do better than that. We all can.

Case Study: Penguin Magic

Hocus has left the building.

Penguin Magic is the sort of company that they invented the internet for.

You may have grown up near a magic shop. There's still one in my little town. Dimly lit, with fake wood paneling, almost certainly with the owner manning the counter. While he may have loved the work, he certainly wasn't very successful.

Today, if you care about magic, you know about Penguin

Magic. It's not the Amazon of magic tricks (because being the Amazon of anything is difficult indeed). Instead, it has grown to significant size by being very different from Amazon and by understanding precisely what its audience wants, knows, and believes.

First, every trick for sale on the site is demonstrated with a video. That video, of course, doesn't reveal how the trick is done, so tension is created. If you want to know the secret, you'll need to buy the trick.

To date, their videos, on the site and on YouTube, have been seen more than a billion times. A billion views with no cost of distribution.

Second, the people who run the site realized that professional magicians rarely buy tricks, because they only need ten or twenty regular tricks in their bag. Since the audience changes every night, they don't worry about repeating themselves.

An amateur, on the other hand, always has the same audience (friends and family) and so he's hooked on constantly changing the routine.

Third, every trick is reviewed in detail. Not reviewed by the knuckleheads who hang out on Yelp or Amazon, but reviewed by other magicians. It's a tough crowd, but one that appreciates good work. There are more than eighty-two thousand product reviews on the site.

As a result, the quality of stock on Penguin cycles very rapidly. Creators see their competitors' work immediately, giving them an impetus to make something even better. Instead of a production cycle measured in years, it might take only a month for an idea to go from notion to product on Penguin. To date, they've carried more than sixteen thousand different items on their site.

Going forward, Penguin continues to invest in building connections not just with the community (they have an email list of tens of thousands of customers) but across it as well. They've hosted three hundred lectures, which have become the TED Talks of magic, as well as going into the field and running nearly a hundred live conventions.

The more magicians learn from each other, the more likely that Penguin will do well.

You're not a cigar-smoking fat cat

You don't work for a soap company. You're not an obsolete industrial marketer.

So why are you acting like one?

Your Kickstarter is nearing its deadline, so sure, you have a good excuse to spam every "influencer" you know, begging for a link. But they ignore you.

You work for a content marketing company, and you obsessively track how many clicks your articles get, even though the crap you write embarrasses you.

You make graphs of how many Instagram followers you have, even though you know everyone else simply buys followers.

You lower your price because people tell you your rates are too high, but it doesn't seem to help.

It's all the same old thing—the industrialized selfish same-old, made modern for a new generation.

Your emergency is not a license to steal my attention. Your insecurity is not a permit to hustle me or my friends.

There's a more effective way. You can do it. It's not easy, but the steps are well lit.

It's time

Time to get off the social media merry-go-round that goes faster and faster but never gets anywhere.

Time to stop hustling and interrupting.

Time to stop spamming and pretending you're welcome.

Time to stop making average stuff for average people while hoping you can charge more than a commodity price.

Time to stop begging people to become your clients, and time to stop feeling bad about charging for your work.

Time to stop looking for shortcuts, and time to start insisting on a long, viable path instead.

CHAPTER TWO

The Marketer Learns to See

In 1983, I was a very young and inexperienced brand manager at Spinnaker, the startup software company I joined after business school. Suddenly, I had millions of dollars in my budget, fancy lunches with ad reps that I didn't ask for, and an urgent need: to get the word out about the software my amazing team had created.

I wasted *all* that ad money. The ads didn't work because the ads were ignored. Somehow, though, the software sold.

Over the years, I've launched dozens and dozens of projects and sold goods and services to businesses and individuals. I've worked with Jay Levinson, the father of Guerrilla Marketing, with Lester Wunderman, the godfather of direct mail, and Bernadette Jiwa, the doyenne of storytelling. My ideas have built billion-dollar companies and raised nearly that much for important charities.

Mostly, the journey has involved noticing what works and trying to understand what doesn't. It's been an ongoing experiment of trial and error (mostly error) with projects and organizations I care about.

And now I have a compass for what marketing is today, about the human condition, and about our culture. This approach is simple, but it's not easy to embrace, because it involves patience, empathy, and respect.

The marketing that has suffused our entire lives is not the marketing that you want to do. The shortcuts using money to buy attention to sell average stuff to average people are an artifact of another time, not the one we live in now.

You can learn to see how human beings dream, decide, and act. And if you help them become better versions of themselves, the ones they seek to be, you're a marketer.

Marketing in five steps

The **first step** is to invent a thing worth making, with a story worth telling, and a contribution worth talking about.

The **second step** is to design and build it in a way that a few people will particularly benefit from and care about.

The **third step** is to tell a story that matches the built-in narrative and dreams of that tiny group of people, the smallest viable market.

The **fourth step** is the one everyone gets excited about: spread the word.

The **last step** is often overlooked: show up—regularly, consistently, and generously, for years and years—to organize and lead and build confidence in the change you seek to make. To earn permission to follow up and to earn enrollment to teach.

As marketers, we get to consistently do the work to help the idea spread from person to person, engaging a tribe as you make change happen.

This Is Marketing: An executive summary

Ideas that spread, win.

Marketers make change happen: for the smallest viable market, and by delivering anticipated, personal, and relevant messages that people actually want to get.

Marketers don't use consumers to solve their company's problem; they use marketing to solve other people's problems. They have the empathy to know that those they seek to serve don't want what the marketer wants, don't believe what they believe, and don't care about what they care about. They probably never will.

At the heart of our culture is our belief in status, in our self-perceived understanding of our role in any interaction, in where we're going next.

We use status roles and our decisions about affiliation and dominion to decide where to go and how to get there.

Persistent, consistent, and frequent stories, delivered to an aligned audience, will earn attention, trust, and action.

Direct marketing is not the same as brand marketing, but they are both based on our decision to make the right thing for the right people.

"People like us do things like this" is how each of us understands culture, and marketers engage with this idea every day.

Ideas move through a slope. They skate through the early

adopters, leap through a chasm, and slog their way to the masses. Sometimes.

Attention is a precious resource since our brains are cluttered with noise. Smart marketers make it easy for those they seek to work with, by helping position the offering in a way that resonates and is memorable.

Most of all, marketing begins (and often ends) with what we do and how we do it, not in all the stuff that comes after the thing is designed and shipped.

Your tactics can make a difference, but your strategy—your commitment to a way of being and a story to be told and a promise to be made—can change everything.

If you want to make change, begin by making culture. Begin by organizing a tightly knit group. Begin by getting people in sync.

Culture beats strategy—so much that culture *is* strategy.

Things marketers know

1. Committed, creative people can change the world (in fact, they're the only ones who do). You can do it right now, and you can make more change than you can possibly imagine.
2. You cannot change everyone; therefore, asking, "Who's it for?" can focus your actions and help you deal with the nonbelievers (in your head and in the outside world).
3. Change is best made with intent. "What's it for?" is the posture of work that matters.

4. Human beings tell themselves stories. Those stories, as far as each of us is concerned, are completely and totally true, and it's foolish to try to persuade them (or us) otherwise.

5. We can group people into stereotyped groups that often (but not always) tell themselves similar stories, groups that make similar decisions based on their perceived status and other needs.

6. What you say isn't nearly as important as what others say about you.

CHAPTER THREE

Marketing Changes People Through Stories, Connections, and Experience

Case Study: VisionSpring—Selling glasses to people who need them

Each person has a story in his or her head, a narrative used to navigate the world. The extraordinary thing is that every person's narrative is different.

A few years ago, I went with a small team to a village in India, trying to understand the challenges that VisionSpring faces in their work.

VisionSpring is a social enterprise that works to get reading glasses to the billion people around the world who need them but don't have them.

When the typical person only lived to thirty or forty years of age, it didn't matter that most people will need reading glasses beginning at age fifty. But as lifespans have increased, more and more people find themselves otherwise healthy and active but unable to work—because they can't read or do close-up work. If you're a weaver or a jeweler or a nurse, working without glasses can be impossible.

VisionSpring's strategy is to produce attractive glasses in bulk at a very low cost, perhaps two dollars a pair. And then, working with local traveling salespeople, they bring the glasses to villages around the world, where they sell them for three dollars or so a pair.

The one-dollar difference between the manufacturing cost and the price is just enough to pay for shipping, for local talent, and for the organization to keep growing.

When we set up our table in the village, many people came to see what was going on. It was the middle of a very hot day and there wasn't much else to do.

The men were wearing traditional Indian work shirts, embroidered, each with a pocket on the front. I could see through the sheer fabric that just about everyone had rupees in their pockets.

So now I knew three things:

1. Based on their age, many of these folks needed glasses. That's simple biology.
2. Many of them weren't wearing or carrying glasses, so they probably didn't own a pair.
3. And most of the people milling around had some money in their pocket. While the glasses might be expensive for someone who only made three dollars a day, each person had access to cash.

One by one, as the villagers came up to our table, we handed each of them a laminated sheet with an eye test on it. The test was set up so that it even worked for people who didn't know how to read, regardless of which languages they spoke.

Then, the villager with the laminated sheet was offered a pair of sample glasses and took the test again. Right there, instantly, he or she could see perfectly. That's how glasses work. It wasn't a new technology for these men and women, or an untrusted one.

After that, the sample glasses were removed and set aside, and the customer was given a mirror and offered a choice of ten different styles. Each was brand new, wrapped in little plastic sleeves. About a third of the people who had come to the table and needed glasses actually bought a pair.

A third.

This mystified me.

I was stunned that 65 percent of the people who needed glasses, who knew they needed glasses, and had money to buy glasses would just walk way.

Putting myself in their shoes, I couldn't imagine making this choice. The supply of glasses was going to disappear in an hour. The price was amazing. The trusted technology worked. What were we doing wrong?

I sat in the sun for an hour, thinking hard about this problem. I felt like all my work as a marketer had led me to this moment.

So I changed just one thing about the process.

One thing that *doubled* the percentage of glasses sold.

Here's what I did: I took all the glasses off the table.

For the rest of the people in line, after they put on the sample glasses, we said, "Here are your new glasses. If they work and you like them, please pay us three dollars. If you don't want them, please give them back."

That's it.

We changed the story from "Here's an opportunity to shop, to look good, to regain your sight, to enjoy the process, to feel ownership from beginning to end" to "Do you want us to take away what you have, or do you want to pay to keep the glasses that are already working for you?"

Desire for gain versus avoidance of loss.

If you've been living in abject poverty, it's hard to imagine the pleasure that more fortunate people take in shopping. To feel the thrill of buying something never bought before.

To go shopping is to take a risk. We risk time and money looking for a new thing, a thing that might be great. And we're able to take that risk because being wrong isn't fatal. Being wrong doesn't cost dinner or a medical checkup.

And if we're wrong, not only will we live another day, but we'll get right back to shopping tomorrow.

On the other hand, with the realization that maybe others didn't think about shopping the way I did, or the way Western opticians did, I saw things differently. Maybe the people we were trying to serve saw shopping for something new as a threat, not as a fun activity.

Most teenagers at the typical suburban mall would bristle at the idea that they didn't get to try on all the glasses, that they didn't get a choice in the matter.

Most of us wouldn't want a pair of used glasses; we'd want

the fancy new ones. Even if "used" simply meant tried on once before. But it's not helpful to imagine that everyone knows what you know, wants what you want, believes what you believe.

My narrative about how to buy glasses isn't better or worse than the one the next villager in line had. My narrative is simply my narrative, and if it's not working, it's arrogant to insist on it.

The way we make things better is by caring enough about those we serve to imagine the story that *they* need to hear. We need to be generous enough to share that story, so they can take action that they'll be proud of.

Consider the SUV

Most people reading this book don't market cars. But most of us have bought one.

The question to ponder is: Why did you buy the one you bought?

Why do people who will never drive off-road buy a ninety thousand-dollar Toyota Land Cruiser?

Why pay extra for the Ludicrous Mode on a Tesla if you never expect (or need) it to go from 0 to 60 mph in less than 3 seconds?

Why put a three thousand-dollar stereo in your car if you only listen to a thirty-dollar clock radio at home?

Even more puzzling: the most popular color for cars varies by the kind of car being purchased.

If we're unwilling to make utility the primary driver of our decisions when buying a fifty thousand-dollar vehicle, what chance does a bottle of perfume or a stick of gum have?

Marketing isn't a race to add more features for less money.

Marketing is our quest to make change on behalf of those we serve, and we do it by understanding the irrational forces that drive each of us.

That riff about the quarter-inch drill bit

Harvard marketing professor Theodore Levitt famously said, "People don't want to buy a quarter-inch drill bit. They want a quarter-inch hole."

The lesson is that the drill bit is merely a feature, a means to an end, but what people truly want is the hole it makes.

But that doesn't go nearly far enough. No one wants a hole.

What people want is the shelf that will go on the wall once they drill the hole.

Actually, what they want is how they'll feel once they see how uncluttered everything is, when they put their stuff on the shelf that went on the wall, now that there's a quarter-inch hole.

But wait . . .

They also want the satisfaction of knowing they did it themselves.

Or perhaps the increase in status they'll get when their spouse admires the work.

Or the peace of mind that comes from knowing that the bedroom isn't a mess, and that it feels safe and clean.

"People don't want to buy a quarter-inch drill bit. They want to feel safe and respected."

Bingo.

People don't want what you make

They want what it will do for them. They want the way it will make them feel. And there aren't that many feelings to choose from.

In essence, most marketers deliver the same feelings. We just do it in different ways, with different services, products, and stories. And we do it for different people in different moments.

If you can bring someone belonging, connection, peace of mind, status, or one of the other most desired emotions, you've done something worthwhile. The thing you sell is simply a road to achieve those emotions, and we let everyone down when we focus on the tactics, not the outcomes. Who's it for and what's it for are the two questions that guide all of our decisions.

Stories, connections, and experiences

The good news is that we don't need to rely on the shiniest, latest digital media shortcut—we have even more powerful, nuanced, and timeless tools at our disposal.

We tell stories. Stories that resonate and hold up over time. Stories that are true, because we made them true with our actions and our products and our services.

We make connections. Humans are lonely, and they want to be seen and known. People want to be part of something. It's safer that way, and often more fun.

We create experiences. Using a product, engaging with a service. Making a donation, going to a rally, calling customer service. Each of these actions is part of the story; each builds a little bit of our connection. As marketers, we can offer these experiences with intent, doing them on purpose.

The entire organization works for and with the marketer, because marketing is all of it. What we make, how we make it, who we make it for. It is the effects and the side effects, the pricing and the profit, all at once.

Market-driven: Who's driving the bus?

Every organization—every project—is influenced by a primary driving force.

Some restaurants are chef-driven. Silicon Valley is often tech-driven. Investment firms in New York are money-driven, focused on the share price or the latest financial manipulation.

The driver, whichever one you choose, is the voice that gets heard the clearest, and the person with that voice is the one who gets to sit at the head of the table.

Often, organizations are marketing-driven. They're slick, focused on the offer, the surface shine, the ability to squeeze out one more dollar.

I'm not really interested in helping you become marketing-driven, because it's a dead end.

The alternative is to be *market-driven*—to hear the market, to listen to it, and even more important, to influence it, to bend it, to make it better.

When you're marketing-driven, you're focused on the latest Facebook data hacks, the design of your new logo, and your Canadian pricing model. On the other hand, when you're market-driven, you think a lot about the hopes and dreams of your customers and their friends. You listen to their frustrations and invest in changing the culture.

Being market-driven lasts.

The myth of rational choice

Microeconomics is based on a demonstrably false assertion: "The rational agent is assumed to take account of available information, probabilities of events, and potential costs and benefits in determining preferences, and to act consistently in choosing the self-determined best choice of action," says Wikipedia.

Of course not.

Perhaps if we average up a large enough group of people, it's possible that in some ways, on average, we might see glimmers of this behavior. But it's not something I'd want you to bet on.

In fact, the bet you'd be better off making is: "When in doubt, assume that people will act according to their current irrational urges, ignoring information that runs counter to their beliefs, trading long-term for short-term benefits and most of all, being influenced by the culture they identify with."

You can make two mistakes here:

1. Assume that the people you're seeking to serve are well-informed, rational, independent, long-term choice makers.

2. Assume that everyone is like you, knows what you know, wants what you want.

I'm not rational and neither are you.

CHAPTER FOUR

The Smallest Viable Market

What change are you trying to make?

It's a simple question, but a loaded one, because it implies that you're responsible. You are an actor with intent, an agent of change, a human being working hard to change other human beings.

It might be your job, it might be your passion, and if you're lucky, it might even be both.

The change might be trivial ("I'm trying to make the market share of OZO brand laundry soap go up 1 percent, and to do that, I need to change some Clorox users to OZO users") or it might be profound ("I'm trying to help the twelve kids in my after-school program realize that they have more potential and skill than the world tells them that they do").

Perhaps it's "I'm going to turn nonvoters into voters," or "I'm going to transform people who seek to dominate into ones who desire affiliation instead."

Regardless of what the specifics are, if you're a marketer,

you're in the business of making change happen. Denying this is a form of hiding; it's more productive to own it instead.

Stumble 1: It's tempting to pick a grandiose, nearly impossible change: "I want to change the face of music education and make it a top priority across the country." Well, sure, that's great, but it's never been done before, not by someone with your resources. I'm a huge fan of game-changing home runs. I love the inspiring stories of people who beat all the odds and changed everything.

But . . .

That's a heavy burden, as well as a convenient excuse in moments of despair. It's no wonder that you're stuck—you're seeking to do the impossible.

Perhaps it makes more sense to begin with a hurdle you can leap. Perhaps it makes sense to be very specific about the change you seek to make, and to make it happen. Then, based on that success, you can replicate the process on ever bigger challenges.

Stumble 2: You want to defend what you're already doing, which is selling what you've already been charged with selling. So you reverse-engineer a "change" that matches that thing, and you load it up with buzzwords that mean nothing to anyone. Here's one I just found: "Activation and engagement for TNT's new thriller that makes a meta-statement about viewer identity."

Really?

On the other hand, here's an example from By the Way Bakery, which my wife founded. It's the largest gluten-free bakery of its kind in the world. Their change? "We want to make sure no one is left out. By offering people gluten-free, dairy-free, and kosher baked goods that happen to be delicious, we let the entire community be part of special family occasions. We change hosts from exclusive to inclusive, and guests from outsiders to insiders."

What promise are you making?

When the marketer shows up with his or her message (in whatever medium), it always takes the form of a promise: "If you do X, you will get Y." That promise is often hidden. It can accidentally be set aside or intentionally camouflaged, but all effective marketing makes a promise.

The promise isn't the same as a guarantee. It's more like, "If this works for you, you're going to discover . . ."

And so we can invite people to our jazz club to have more than a pleasant evening. Or promise that if they listen to our tapes, they'll begin a spiritual journey. Or that our special kind of cheese will transport them to Old Italy . . . We're not talking about slogans here, but these slogans give you an insight into the kind of promise I'm talking about.

"They laughed when I sat down at the piano . . . but when I began to play . . ." is a promise about status.

"Roll Tide!" is a promise about dominance.

"Choosy mothers choose Jif," is a promise about status and respect.

"I pledge allegiance . . ." is a promise about belonging.

"The Earth needs a good lawyer" is a promise about affiliation and justice.

Your promise is directly connected to the change you seek to make, and it's addressed to the people you seek to change.

Who are you seeking to change?

As soon as you ask yourself about the change you seek to make, it becomes quite clear that you have no chance of changing *everyone*. Everyone is a lot of people. Everyone is too diverse, too enormous, and too indifferent for you to have a chance at changing.

So, you need to change *someone*. Or perhaps a group of someones.

Which ones?

We don't care if they all look the same, but it would be really helpful if you had some way to group them together. Do they share a belief? A geography? A demographic, or, more likely, a psychographic?

Can you pick them out of a crowd? What makes them different from everyone else and similar to each other?

Throughout this book, we'll return to this essential question: "Who's it for?" It has a subtle but magic power, the ability to shift the product you make, the story you tell, and where you tell it. Once you're clear on "who it's for," then doors begin to open for you.

Here's a simple example. Both Dunkin' Donuts and Starbucks sell coffee. But for the first two decades of its existence,

Starbucks didn't try to sell coffee to people who bought from Dunkin', and vice versa.

While there are external hints about the two groups (in Boston, you would find more taxi drivers and construction workers at a typical Dunkin' Donuts than you would at a Starbucks) the real distinction wasn't external but internal. Starbucks set out to serve someone with a very precise set of beliefs about coffee, time, money, community, opportunity, and luxury—and by obsessing over this group of someones, Starbucks built a brand for the ages.

Worldviews and personas

But *which* market?

Which people?

If you have to choose a thousand people to become your true fans, who should you choose?

Begin by choosing people based on what they dream of, believe, and want, not based on what they look like. In other words, use psychographics instead of demographics.

Just as you can group people by the color of their eyes or the length of their ring fingers, you can group them based on the stories they tell themselves. Cognitive linguist George Lakoff calls these clumps *worldviews*.

A worldview is the shortcut, the lens each of us uses when we see the world. It's our assumptions and biases and yes, stereotypes about the world around us. Loyal Fox News viewers have a worldview. So do fox hunters. So do people who show up at the midnight screening of *The Rocky Horror Picture Show.* Everyone deserves to be treated as an individual, with dignity and respect for their choices. But as marketers, we must begin with a worldview, and invite people who share that worldview to join us. "I made this" is a very different statement than, "What do you want?"

We can make pretty good assumptions about how someone will react or respond to a piece of news or a work of art if we have evidence about their worldview.

When Ron Johnson was hired as CEO of JCPenney in 2011, one of his first acts was to end the constant stream of discounts and urgent sales that the store was always pitching to its customers. Johnson took that action based on *his* worldview, on his bias about how to shop. He didn't think it was possible that a quality retailer, a store he'd like to shop in, would be constantly pitching clearances, coupons, and discounts, and so he tried to transform JCPenney into *his* kind of store. As a result, sales plummeted by more than 50 percent.

Coming from his previous position as senior vice president of retail operations at Apple, Johnson saw the world of retail through a lens of elegance, of quiet, mutual respect. He was a luxury goods buyer, and he liked selling luxury goods as well. As a result of his worldview, he abandoned Penney's true fans: people who loved the sport of bargain hunting. Or the urgency. People whose worldviews differed from his. Penney's customers were playing a game, one that made them feel like they were winning.

Yes, we're typecasting—willfully exaggerating people's attitudes and beliefs in order to serve them better.

A convenient shortcut in this exercise is to identify the different personas we might encounter. There's Bargain Bill, who's playing a sport when he shops at the same time he wrestles with his narrative about money. And there's Hurried Henry, who is always looking for a shortcut and is rarely willing to wait in line, read the directions, or think it through, at least not when he's traveling for business. Next to him in line, though, is Careful Karla, who's suspicious of the cab driver, sure that she's going to get ripped off by the desk clerk, and would never drink out of the hotel mini bar.

Everyone has a problem, a desire, and a narrative.

Who will you seek to serve?

Forcing a focus

The relentless pursuit of mass will make you boring, because mass means average, it means the center of the curve, it requires you to offend no one and satisfy everyone. It will lead to compromises and generalizations. Begin instead with the *smallest viable market*. What's the minimum number of people you would need to influence to make it worth the effort?

If you could only change thirty people, or three thousand people, you'd want to be choosy about which people. If you were limited in scale, you'd focus your energy on the makeup of the market instead.

When the Union Square Cafe opened in New York, its founder, Danny Meyer, knew that he could only serve six hundred people a day. That's all the dining room could serve. If you can only delight six hundred people, the best way to begin is by choosing *which* six hundred people. Choose the people who want what you're offering. Choose the people most open to hearing your message. Choose the people who will tell the right other people . . . The magic of Union Square Cafe wasn't the real estate (it was in a lousy neighborhood when it opened) or in the famous chef (they didn't have one). No, the magic was in the guts it took to carefully curate the customers. Choose the people you serve, choose your future.

The smallest viable market is the focus that, ironically and delightfully, leads to your growth.

Specific is a kind of bravery

Specific means accountable.

It worked or it didn't.

It matched or it didn't.

It spread or it didn't.

Are you hiding behind *everyone* or *anyone*?

You'll never be able to serve everyone, which is comforting, since you're less likely to be disappointed when it doesn't happen.

But what if you committed to the smallest viable audience? What if you were specific about who you were seeking to serve and precisely what change you were trying to make?

Organize your project, your life, and your organization around the minimum. What's the smallest market you can survive on?

Once you've identified the scale, then find a corner of the market that can't wait for your attention. Go to their extremes. Find a position on the map where you, and you alone, are the perfect answer. Overwhelm this group's wants and dreams and desires with your care, your attention, and your focus. Make change happen. Change that's so profound, people can't help but talk about it.

Lean entrepreneurship is built around the idea of the minimal viable product. Figure out the simplest useful version of your product, engage with the market, and then improve and repeat.

What people miss about this idea is the word *viable*. No fair shipping junk. It doesn't help to release something that doesn't work yet.

When we combine these ideas, we can think small and think quickly. Our agile approach to the market combined with a relentless focus on those we seek to serve means that we're more likely to be of service.

Entrepreneur and Silicon Valley pioneer Steve Blank introduced a focus on the customer as the only project of a startup. Customer development is the act of gaining traction with customers, of finding a fit between what you make and what they want. This traction is worth far more than fancy technology or expensive marketing. That, and only that, separates successful projects from unsuccessful ones. Are there people in the world who want you to succeed so badly that they're willing to pay you to produce the change you seek to make?

Everything gets easier when you walk away from the hubris of *everyone*. Your work is not for everyone. It's only for those who signed up for the journey.

Shun the nonbelievers!

There's a filter bubble. It's easy to surround ourselves with nothing but news we agree with. We can spend our days believing that everyone shares our worldview, believes what we believe, and wants what we want.

Until we start marketing to the masses.

When we seek to serve the largest possible audience, that audience will turn us down. The chorus of "no" will become deafening. And the feedback may be direct, personal, and specific.

In the face of so much rejection, it's easy to sand off the edges and fit in. Fit in all the way. Fit in more than anyone else.

Resist.

It's not for them.

It's for the smallest viable audience, the folks you originally set out to serve.

Where does love lie?

Pioneering technology journalist Clay Shirky understood how community-driven software changes everything: "We have lived in this world where little things are done for love and big things for money. Now we have Wikipedia. Suddenly big things can be done for love."

But it doesn't end with software.

The goal of the smallest viable audience is to find people who will understand you and will fall in love with where you hope to take them.

Loving you is a way of expressing themselves. Becoming part of your movement is an expression of who they are.

That love leads to traction, to engagement, and to evangelism. That love becomes part of their identity, a chance to do something that feels right. To express themselves through their contributions, their actions, and the badge they wear.

You can't hope that everyone will feel this way, but you can do your work for the people who do.

"Winner take all" rarely is

Even in a democracy, a situation where second place rarely pays off, the idea of "everyone" is a mistake.

I was talking with two congressional campaign organizers, and they kept talking about getting the message out to everyone, connecting with everyone, getting everyone to the polls.

I did a little research and discovered that in the last primary in that district, only twenty thousand people voted, which means that in a contested primary, getting five thousand people to the polls is the difference between winning and losing. The district has 724,000 residents; five thousand people is less than 1 percent of that.

There's a very big difference between five thousand and "everyone." And for your work, five thousand of the right people might well be more than enough.

A simple one-word transformation

Now that you see that your work is to make change, and that you can do it by identifying who you want to change, earning enrollment, and educating on the way to that change, let's transform how you can describe those you're changing.

Perhaps instead of talking about prospects and customers, we could call them your "students" instead.

Where are your students?

What will they benefit from learning?

Are they open to being taught?

What will they tell others?

This isn't the student–teacher relationship of testing and compliance. And it's not the power dynamic of sexism or racism. It's the student–mentor relationship of enrollment and choice and care.

If you had a chance to teach us, what would we learn?

If you had a chance to learn, what would you like to be taught?

Coloring the ocean purple

There's a dangerous prank that relies on thief-detector dye. This dye, sold as a powder, is quite bright and a tiny bit goes a long way. Once the powder touches the moisture on your skin, it blooms into a bright purple and won't easily wash off.

Drop a teaspoon of it into a swimming pool, and all the water in the pool will become permanently bright purple. But if you drop it in the ocean, no one will notice.

When you seek to share your best work—your best story, your shot at change—it helps if it's likely to spread. It helps if it's permanent. But even if it's extraordinary, it's not going to make a difference if you drop it in the ocean.

That doesn't mean you give up hope.

It means you walk away from the ocean and look for a large swimming pool.

That's enough to make a difference. Begin there, with obsessive focus. Once it works, find another swimming pool. Even better, let your best customers spread the idea.

"It's not for you"

We're not supposed to say that. We're certainly not supposed to *want* to say that.

But we must.

"It's not for you" shows the ability to respect someone enough that you're not going to waste their time, pander to them, or insist that they change their beliefs. It shows respect for those you seek to serve, to say to them, "I made this for you. Not for the other folks, but for *you*."

Two sides of the same coin.

It's the freedom to ignore the critics who don't get the joke, the privilege of polishing your story for those that most need to hear it. . . . This is where you will find work that you can be proud of.

Because it doesn't matter what people you're not seeking to serve think. What matters is whether you've changed the people who trust you, the people who have connected with you, the people you seek to serve.

We know that every best-selling book on Amazon has at least a few one-star reviews. It's impossible to create work that both matters *and* pleases everyone.

The comedian's dilemma

One of the great comics of our time is booked for a gig in New York City. His agent isn't paying attention, though.

The comic shows up at the club; he's in a good mood. He brings his best material. He's up there, working the room, and no one is laughing.

Not a peep.

He's bombing.

After the show, he's beating himself up, thinking of quitting comedy altogether.

Then he discovers that the audience is an Italian tour group, and no one understands English.

"It's not for you."

It's entirely possible that your work isn't as good as it needs to be. But it's also possible that you failed to be clear about who it was for in the first place.

The simple marketing promise

Here's a template, a three-sentence marketing promise you can run with:

> My product is for people who believe _____.
>
> I will focus on people who want _____.
>
> I promise that engaging with what I make will help you get _____.

And you thought that all you were here to do was sell soap.

Case Study: The Open Heart Project

Susan Piver was a respected teacher of meditation. She had written a *New York Times* best-selling book, and her classes were well attended. She, like many before her, had a practice and a small following.

What she found, though, was that after a retreat, people from out of town would ask, "How do we find a local teacher we can connect with to continue our practice?"

To meet this need, she decided to build an online meditation center, a sangha.

A few years later, the sangha has more than twenty thousand members. Most of them get periodic updates and video lessons, and pay nothing for the interactions. Some, though, are more deeply connected. They pay a subscription fee and engage with their teacher (and with each other) as often as every day.

How did she get to twenty thousand? Not in one fell swoop. In thousands of small swoops.

After just a few years, this small project has become the largest meditation community in the world. With just one full-time staff member, it connects and inspires thousands of people.

There are countless meditation instructors in the United States, all of whom have access to a laptop as connected to the world as Susan's is. How did the Open Heart Project make such an impact?

1. Start with empathy to see a real need. Not an invented one, not "How can I start a business?" but, "What would matter here?"
2. Focus on the smallest viable market: "How few people could find this indispensable and still make it worth doing?"
3. Match the worldview of the people being served. Show up in the world with a story that they want to hear, told in a language they're eager to understand.
4. Make it easy to spread. If every member brings in one more member, within a few years, you'll have more members than you can count.

5. Earn, and keep, the attention and trust of those you serve.
6. Offer ways to go deeper. Instead of looking for members for your work, look for ways to do work for your members.
7. At every step along the way, create and relieve tension as people progress in their journeys toward their goals.
8. Show up, often. Do it with humility, and focus on the parts that work.

CHAPTER FIVE

In Search of "Better"

The Beer Advocate website lists 250 beers that have earned more than 3,400 ratings each. Each beer is someone's favorite. It's possible that there are thousands of beers in the United States that are someone's favorite.

How can that be? Because taste matters. Everyone else is wrong.

When a marketer arrives and says, "This is better," he's wrong.

He actually means, "This is better for someone and it might be better for you."

Empathy is at the heart of marketing

People don't believe what you believe.

They don't know what you know.

They don't want what you want.

It's true, but we'd rather not accept this.

Sonder is defined as that moment when you realize that everyone around you has an internal life as rich and as conflicted as yours.

Everyone has noise in their heads.

Everyone thinks that they are right, and that they have suffered affronts and disrespect at the hands of others.

Everyone is afraid. And everyone realizes that they are also lucky.

Everyone has an impulse to make things better, to connect and to contribute.

Everyone wants something that they can't possibly have. And if they could have it, they'd discover that they didn't really want it all along.

Everyone is lonely, insecure, and a bit of a fraud. And everyone cares about something.

As a marketer, then, we have little chance of doing marketing to others, in insisting that they get with our program, that they realize how hard we've worked, how loud the noise is in our heads, how important our cause is . . .

It's so much more productive to dance with them instead.

A million-dollar bargain

Consider the plight of the nonprofit fundraiser. She's trying to raise a million dollars to pay for a new building on campus. Every time she's meeting with a foundation or a philanthropist and an objection is raised, she says to herself, "You're right, that's a crazy amount of money. I'd never give a million dollars to charity—I have enough trouble paying my rent."

And so the donation doesn't get made.

Empathy changes this dynamic. Because the donation isn't for her, it's for the donor.

It's for the donor who says to himself, "This million-dollar donation is a bargain. I'm going to get at least two million dollars' worth of joy, status, and satisfaction out of this decision." And that's okay. It's the way choice works.

Everything that we purchase—every investment, every trinket, every experience—is a bargain. That's why we bought it. Because it was worth more than what we paid for it. Otherwise, we wouldn't buy it.

Which means, going back to the hapless fundraiser, that if you're unwilling to have empathy for the narrative of the person you seek to serve, you're stealing.

You're stealing because you're withholding a valuable option. You're keeping someone from understanding how much they'll benefit from what you've created . . . such a significant benefit that it's a bargain.

If they understand what's on offer and choose not to buy it, then it's not for them. Not today, not at this price, not with that structure.

That's okay too.

Thinking about "better"

It's tempting to decide that there's a transitive relationship, that A > B > C. This works, for example, with length. A ruler is longer than a thumb and a thumb is longer than a peppercorn, and therefore a ruler is longer than a peppercorn.

But linear comparisons don't make sense when we're building stories and opportunities for humans.

An Hermès bag is more expensive than a Louis Vuitton bag, which is more expensive than one from Coach. But that doesn't mean that the Hermès bag is "better." It merely means that it's more expensive, which is just one of the many things that someone might care about.

Expense might be easy to measure, but it's never clear that more of it is always better.

What about more subjective categories like "stylish" or "fashionable" or "status"? Suddenly, it's not linear. Not easy to measure. Not clear at all what better means.

Better isn't up to you

There are more than 250 models of motorcycles available for sale in Cleveland. Can you name them? No one can, not even a motorcycle collector.

And the same thing is true for ketchup, for insurance brokers, for churches.

So, how do we process this, remember this, choose a product?

We remember the best one.

Best for what?

And that's the key question. *Best for us.*

If we care about sustainability and price, then our brain has a slot for our favorite brand, and it's the one that's the best at sustainability and price. No surprise.

But our neighbor, the one who cares far more about status within the group and luxury, has a very different brand in mind.

Which is not surprising, because we're humans, not machines.

Your job as a marketer is to find a spot on the map with edges that (some) people want to find. Not a selfish, unique selling proposition, done to maximize your market share, but a generous beacon, a signal flare sent up so that people who are looking for you can easily find you.

We're this, not that.

The marketing of dog food

Dog food *must* be getting better. More nutritious and of course, delicious.

Americans spent more than twenty-four billion dollars on dog food last year. The average price has skyrocketed, and so has the gourmet nature of ingredients, like sweet potatoes, elk, and free-range bison.

And yet, I've never seen a dog buy dog food.

Have you?

Dog food might be getting more delicious as it gets more expensive, but we actually have no idea. We have no clue whether dogs enjoy it more, because we're not dogs.

But we can be sure that dog *owners* like it more.

Because dog food is for dog owners. It's for the way it makes them feel, the satisfaction of taking care of an animal that responds with loyalty and affection, the status of buying a luxury good, and the generosity of sharing it.

Some dog owners want to spend more on the dog food they buy. Some want gluten-free dog food, loaded with high-value placebos.

But let's not get confused about who all this innovation is for. It's not for the dogs.

It's for us.

A marketer for a dog food company might decide that the secret of more dog food sales is to make a food that tastes better. But that requires understanding how a dog thinks, which is awfully difficult.

It turns out that the right formula is to make a dog food that dog owners want to buy.

The purpose of this example isn't to help you market dog food better. It's to understand that there's almost always a disconnect between performance and appeal. That the engineer's choice of the best price/performance combination is rarely the market's choice.

There are two voices in our heads. There's the dog's voice, the one that doesn't have many words, but knows what it wants. And there's the owner's voice, which is nuanced, contradictory, and complex. It's juggling countless inputs and is easily distracted.

Like the dog owner who is choosing based on a hundred factors (but not taste), the people you seek to serve care about a range of inputs and emotions, not simply a contest for who's the cheapest.

Choose your extremes and you choose your market. And vice versa.

Early adopters are not adapters: They crave the new

Early adopters are at the start of the marketer's journey. But it's important not to think of them as *adapters*. Adapters figure out how to get along when the world changes. They're not happy about it, but they figure it out.

The early adopters are different. They are neophiliacs— addicted to the new. They get a thrill from discovery, they enjoy the tension of "This might not work," and they get pleasure from bragging about their discoveries. The neophiliacs are very forgiving of missteps from those who seek to innovate with them, and incredibly unforgiving after the initial thrill of discovery wears off.

That relentless desire for better is precisely why they're always looking for something new. You can't be perfect in the eyes of an early adopter; the best you can do is be interesting.

In your work as a marketer, you'll be torn between two poles. Sometimes, you'll be busy creating interesting new work for people who are easily bored. And sometimes, you'll be trying to build products and services that last, that can extend beyond the tiny group of neophiliacs and reach and delight the rest of the market.

There's almost nothing a marketer can do that shouldn't be prefaced with that distinction. The magic question is: *Who's it for?*

The people you seek to serve—what do they believe? What do they want?

An aside about the reptile people
who are secretly running things

Professor Roland Imhoff of the Johannes Gutenberg University in Mainz, Germany, wanted to understand what makes some people choose their beliefs.

In particular, he's been studying a particular kind of outlier: the conspiracy theorist. Since we know that conspiracy theories aren't factual, why are they so appealing to some people? And which people?

In one study he cited, it was found that many people who believe that Lady Diana is still alive, having faked her own death, *also* believe that she was murdered. And in a similar study, people who believe that Osama bin Laden was dead before the Navy Seals arrived at his compound are also likely to report that he's still alive.

The facts aren't at issue here; they can't be. What's happening is that these theorists are taking comfort in their standing as outliers and *they're searching for a feeling, not a logical truth*. Imhoff writes, "Adherence to conspiracy theory might not always be the result of some perceived lack of control, but rather a deep-seated need for uniqueness."

In Imhoff's study, he presented American conspiracy theorists with made-up "facts" about a conspiracy regarding smoke detectors in Germany. When he told this group that 81 percent of the German population believed the theory of the conspiracy, they weren't nearly as interested or enthusiastic as when they heard that only 19 percent of the population supported the theory.

By rooting for the overlooked underdog, the conspiracy theorist engages with his desired emotion, that of feeling unique, a brave truth-teller, the outsider.

This group doesn't see themselves as kooks. Each member doesn't have a unique theory, all alone in a field. Instead, they seek to be part of a *small* group, a minority group, an outspoken group that can take solace in each other while the outside world ignores them. They can find this feeling every time they hang out with the other reptile-spotters.

That's not that big a leap from the countless micro-tribes that so many early adopters belong to.

Sooner or later, each of us becomes (for a while) the kind of person who believes in the reptile people that control the earth. We're seeking our own little pocket of uniqueness.

Humility and curiosity

A marketer is curious about other people. She wonders about what others are struggling with, what makes them tick. She's fascinated by their dreams and their beliefs.

And she has the humility to embrace the lack of time and attention that her audience wrestles with every day.

People aren't eager to pay you with their attention. The fact that you bought an ad doesn't earn you something that priceless.

Instead, we can hope that people might voluntarily *trade* their attention. Trade it for something they need or want. Trade it because they're genuinely interested. Trade it because they trust you to keep your promise.

Not everyone will be interested. But if you do your job right, enough people will.

This is the lock and the key. You're not running around grabbing every conceivable lock to try out your key. Instead, you're finding people (the lock), and since you are curious about their dreams and desires, you will create a key just for them, one they'll happily trade attention for.

A lifeguard doesn't have to spend much time pitching to the drowning person. When you show up with a life buoy, if the drowning person understands what's at stake, you don't have to run ads to get them to hold on to it.

Case Study: *Be More Chill*—More than one way to make a hit

Two years after almost no one went to see this poorly reviewed musical debut in New Jersey, its soundtrack showed up on the *Billboard* Top 10 original cast album chart. More than a hundred million streams after it was first recorded, *Be More Chill* is the hit musical that you can't see (yet).

Except for *Hamilton*, this is the most beloved musical of its time, spawning fan fiction, illustrated video animatics, and high school productions.

This phenomenon happened without a Broadway debut. Without the risk and time and committee meetings. And most definitely without strong reviews after opening night. Charles

Isherwood wrote in the *New York Times*: "predictable in its contours . . . stale . . . boilerplate . . ."

The thing is, it wasn't a play for Isherwood or any of the other critics. It was aimed squarely at the new generation that has adopted it. And talked about it. And shared it. A fan named Claudia Cacace in Naples, Italy, drew some of the video animation, which was seen by Dove Calderwood in Idaho Falls, Idaho, who hired her to draw some more. And so it spreads.

At a recent café performance and meet and greet in New York (the meet and greet lasted for several hours), fans came from all over the world to meet the creators. And, just as important, each other.

It should come as no surprise that there will be a new run of the musical. Off-Broadway this time.

What's a car for?

More specifically, what's a teenager's first car for?

It's not simply a need for transport. After all, when the teenager was fifteen, he didn't have that much of a transport problem. And plenty of teenagers make it through the college years without a car. This is a want, not a need.

Few purchases cause more change than this one, and in this case, we're seeing different changes for different people.

For the teenager, a car enables a change from dependent child to independent adult.

That's a shift in status, in perception, and in power. It's far bigger than four wheels.

For the parent, it causes a change from dominion over someone to offering freedom and responsibility. And it leads to significant discussions about safety, about control, and about status.

What will the neighbors say? What will we tell ourselves about safety? About independence, opportunity, and coddling?

All of these changes are at the heart of the car decision. When the designer, the marketer, and the salesperson see these changes at work, they provide more value, because they can design with these issues in mind.

Too many choices

Old-fashioned industrial marketing is built around the person who pays for the ads. It's done *to* the customer, not *for* him or her. Traditional marketing uses pressure, bait and switch, and any available coercive methods to make the sale—to land the client, to get the money, to sign on the line that is dotted.

When the customer has no choice but to listen to you and engage with you, when there are only three TV channels, only one store in town, only a few choices, the race to the bottom is the race worth winning.

But the newly empowered consumer has discovered that what looks like clutter to the marketer feels like choice. They've come to realize that there are an infinite number of choices, an endless parade of alternatives. For the marketer, it's like trying to sell sand in a desert.

A million books published every year.

More than five hundred kinds of battery chargers on Amazon.

More coaches, courses, and clubs than they could ever consider, never mind hire or join.

Surrounded by this tsunami of choice, most of it offered by folks who are simply selfish, the consumer has made an obvious choice. Walk away.

Positioning as a service

In a world of choice, where we have too little time, too little space, and too many options, how do we choose?

It's easier for those we seek to serve simply to shut down and not even try to solve their problems. If it feels like any choice is going to be wrong, it's better to do nothing. If the world is filled with claims and hype, people believe none of it.

Marketers can choose to stand for *something*. Instead of saying "You can choose anyone, and we're anyone," the marketer can begin with an audience worth serving, begin with their needs and wants and dreams, and then build something for that audience.

This involves going to extremes.

Finding an edge.

Standing for something, not everything.

The method: draw a simple XY grid.

Every available alternative can be graphed on the grid. (I'm not calling them competitors yet, and you'll see why.) All the potato chips in a given supermarket. All the types of care for a bad back. All the spiritual institutions in a small town.

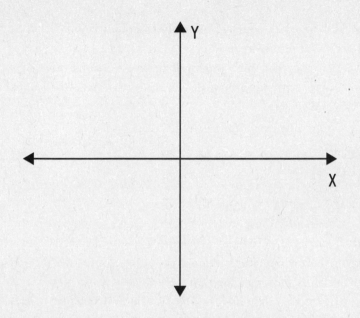

Pick two axes. One is arrayed horizontally (X) and one vertically (Y).

For each axis, choose something that people care about. It could be something like convenience, price, healthfulness, performance, popularity, skill level, or efficacy.

For example, there are six ways to get some diamonds across town. On one axis we have speed, and on the other we have security. It turns out that both an armored car and the postal service will happily insure a small envelope of diamonds, but one will take a long time and the other will take an afternoon.

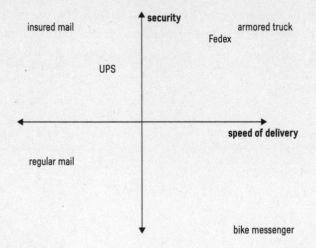

If you don't care about security, a bike messenger is even faster. And if you don't care about speed or security, well, a stamp will work fine.

The magic of the XY positioning of extremes is that it clarifies that each option might be appropriate, depending on what you seek. Can you see how this chart would be totally different if the axes were changed to convenience, cost, environmental impact, or scalability?

The same approach can work for potato chips (expensive, local, air baked, flavored, extra thick, cheap, etc.) or for Walmart, Zales, and Tiffany (price, convenience, status, scarcity). Or a cruise ship and a private jet. Or perhaps a Ford, a Tesla, and a McLaren. We're not so much interested in features as we are in the emotions that those features evoke.

Here are some axes for you to choose from. Because you know your space far better than I do, I'm sure you can come up with some others.

Speed	Imminence
Price	Visibility
Performance	Trendiness
Ingredients	Privacy
Purity	Professionalism
Sustainability	Difficulty
Obviousness	Elitism
Maintenance costs	Danger
Safety	Experimental
Edginess	Limited
Distribution	Incomplete
Network effect	

After you pick an attribute with two extremes for the X-axis, find a different attribute and use it for the Y-axis. Plot the options your customer has on this chart.

Now you have a map of how the alternatives stack up. A map that a busy human being can use to find the solution to her problem.

Some potato chips are marketed as healthy and organic.

Others as traditional and satisfying. Still others as cheap and widely consumed.

Marketers have been doing this forever. When David Ogilvy and Rosser Reeves (and probably Don Draper) were making ads in the 1950s, they figured out a hole in the market and then simply invented claims and features that would fill that hole. So, one soap is for people who want purity, while another is for people who care about not having dry skin. It didn't matter if the soaps were the same, since they were "positioning" themselves. And then as marketing pioneers Jack Trout and Al Ries pushed it further, challenging marketers to position the competition into a corner while you worked to keep a spot to yourself.

This is all fine, but it doesn't hold up over time, not in a hyper-competitive world. Instead, we can think of the quest for the edges as:

- Claims that are true, that we continually double down on in all our actions.

- Claims that are generous, that exist as a service to the customer.

The local music teacher, for example, needs to begin not merely by saying "I'm local," because, as we all know, there are other teachers just as local. Moreover, "I'm pretty good at teaching" and "I won't yell at your kid" are hardly attributes worth talking about.

On the other hand, if he chooses "I'm serious, my students

are serious, and this is about rigor" as one axis, and "My students win competitions" as the other one, suddenly you have a teacher worth driving to, a teacher worth paying extra for.

Is this the teacher I wish I'd had growing up? Absolutely not. It's not for me. But for the parent who views the practice room as a form of character-building, and for the student who sees music as a competition, this is precisely what they wanted.

And now the teacher has his work cut out for him. Because he does, in fact, have to be more rigorous and professional than other teachers. He does have to make the difficult decision of expelling students who aren't serious enough. And he has to persevere enough with his corps of students that they actually do win competitions.

A few blocks away, a different teacher can take a totally different spot on the map. She can work with the whole student, focusing on the experience, not the notes. She can refuse to enter competitions but instead build a practice based on connection and generosity.

Both teachers treat different people differently. They don't compete; they're simply on the same board.

Choose your axes, choose your future

When you look at the list of available attributes, it's tempting to pick the ones that most people care about. After all, it's hard work to claim an edge, and to pick one that few people care about seems foolish. Better, we think, to pick the popular one.

If you do, you'll certainly be choosing a crowded quadrant. And without the magic of advertising, it's very difficult to grow in a quadrant that's crowded. Your customer doesn't know what to do, so he does nothing.

The alternative is to build your own quadrant. To find two axes that have been overlooked. To build a story, a true story, that keeps your promise, that puts you in a position where you are the clear and obvious choice.

Everyone else, the average or hard-working brands that picked the average or popular axes—they're all lumped together. They are Oldsmobile and Plymouth and Chevrolet and the rest of the lumpenproletariat.

You, on the other hand, have gone out on a limb, one that belongs to you, and maybe, just maybe, there are underserved customers out there who can't wait to find you, connect with you, and spread the word.

So many choices

Software, perfume, insurance, candidates, authors, devices, coaches, charities, and retailers—there's a brand everywhere you look. If you could only pick one brand to put next to each of the following emotions, one brand that you'd choose to help you feel a certain way, which brand would you pick?

Safe   Powerful

Beautiful   Worthy

Responsible   Connected

Smart   Hip

If the marketers have done a good job, they have made these choices easy for you.

People are waiting for you

They just don't know it yet.

They're waiting for the edge you will stake out, the one that they can imagine but don't expect.

They're waiting for the connection you will offer. The ability to see and be seen.

And they're waiting for the tension of the possible, the ability to make things better.

Your freedom

You have the freedom to change your story. You can live a different one, one that's built around those you seek to serve.

You have the freedom to change how you spend your day. You can outsource the tasks and find the guts to do emotional labor instead. You can go out on a limb and do what others aren't doing.

The most frustrated marketers I know are the ones who take it as a given that because they are in industry x, they have no freedom.

And so real estate brokers hustle for listings and do precisely what the other brokers do.

And so pharma marketers run slightly generic ads and skirt the line in influencing doctors, instead of realizing how many options they actually have.

And so we get on the Facebook merry-go-round, boosting our posts, counting our followers, and creating ever more content in the hope of being noticed. There are so many other ways to make an impact and earn trust.

Much of what we take for granted in our marketing toolbox was considered a risky innovation just a few generations ago. It's worth discarding the cruft that we built and replacing it with more generous tools.

The freedom of better

After the refrigerator was popularized, there wasn't a good reason to continue hiring the ice delivery man. It wasn't better worth paying for.

After the supermarket took off, it got harder to justify the work of the milkman.

And now we can all take advantage of the huge shifts in what it takes to do what we used to do (it's all at our fingertips now, right?) and use that leverage to redefine better.

Because better is what our market is waiting for.

Consider the real estate broker. He used to hoard data. If you didn't hire a broker, you had no information about what you were looking for. Today, in a world where Zillow has 110 million homes listed, the home shopper is likely to have access to at least as much information as the broker does.

If the goal is to defend the status quo, to be a chokepoint, it's going to require an exhausting sprint, one that tries to keep ahead of an ever-quickening technology and information flow.

But what would better look like? *Not for you, but for the customer?*

This shift is true for many of us. So much of the work is networked, automated, and reliable now. I needed a team of eight engineers and a budget of millions of dollars to send emails to a million people in 1994. Today, anyone can do it for nine dollars a month using Feedblitz.

A decade ago, it took a dedicated team of publishers, print brokers, and sales reps to get a book to be available nationwide. Now a Kindle book can be published by one smart person with a digital file.

We made the "doing" easier, which is precisely why we need to outsource that part of our job and focus all our energy onto the hard work of making change happen.

One last thing about sonder

We're not faking our points of view, our dreams, and our fears. And neither are you.

In politics, there's a long history of people believing that those on the "other side" don't really mean what they say. That Barry Goldwater and Jane Fonda were just putting on a show. That atheists really, deep down, believe in God, and that evangelicals are mostly trying to make a point, not express their actual beliefs.

The same goes for Mac users versus those who favor the Linux command line, or for math geeks versus those who insist that they can't do math.

We assume that someone can't possibly believe that they can't do math. Or they can't possibly support that insane policy. Or eat food like that on purpose.

We're not faking it. Your customers aren't faking it. Those who prefer your competition aren't either.

If we can accept that people have embraced who they have become, it gets a lot easier to dance with them. Not transform them, not get them to admit that they were wrong. Simply to dance with them, to have a chance to connect with them, to add our story to what they see and add our beliefs to what they hear.

CHAPTER SIX

Beyond Commodities

Problem first

Effective marketers don't begin with a solution, with the thing that makes them more clever than everyone else. Instead, we begin with a group we seek to serve, a problem they seek to solve, and a change they seek to make.

There's a gap in the market where your version of better can make a welcome change happen. Not a tactical change. Not a quarter-inch hole, or even a quarter-inch drill bit. No, we can change someone on an emotional level.

Our calling is to make a difference. A chance to make things better for those we seek to serve.

Yes, you have a calling: to serve people in a way that they need (or want). The opportunity is for each of us to choose a path and follow that, not for your own benefit, but because of what it can produce for others.

Does it work?

In 1906, the precursor of the FDA was formed to combat products that were fundamentally dangerous. Anger about products like Berry's Freckle Ointment, a cosmetic that was quite likely to make you sick, or LashLure, which caused more than a dozen forms of blindness, moved the government to act.

As much as fifty years later, product quality was still a crapshoot. Who knew when your car was going to break down?

Today we take it all for granted. FedEx actually does deliver more than 99 percent of its packages on time. Cars don't spontaneously break. Makeup doesn't often cause blindness. Your web browser rarely crashes, the electricity almost never goes out, and air travel has never been safer.

And yet we still talk about being very good at our craft as if it's some sort of bizarre exception.

Plenty of people are good at what you do. Very good at it. Perhaps as good at it as you are.

Full credit for the work you've done and the skill you possess. But it's not enough.

Quality, the quality of meeting specifications, is required but no longer sufficient.

If you can't deliver quality yet, this book isn't much help to you. If you can, great, congratulations. Now, let's set that aside for a minute and remember that nearly everyone else can too.

The commodity suckout

If you make something that others make, if it's something we can find on Upwork, on Amazon, or Alibaba, you've got pain.

It's the pain of knowing that if you raise your price enough to earn a decent return on the effort you're putting into your work, we'll just go somewhere else and buy it cheaper.

When the price of everything is a click away, we're not afraid to click.

Selling ice cream on the beach in the summer is easy. Raising people's expectations, engaging in their hopes and dreams, helping them see further—that's the difficult work we signed up for.

From now on, your customers know more than you do about your competitors. And so your commodity work, no matter how much effort you put into it, is not enough.

"You can choose anyone, and we're anyone"

Imagine a shoeshine stand downtown.

One approach is to find the best location you can afford and offer to shine the shoes of anyone who needs a shoeshine.

There are problems with this.

First, if anyone can shine shoes the way you shine shoes, then a competitor down the street will take half of your business—more, if they cut their price.

Second, and more important, no one needs their shoes shined. It's a want, not a need.

And why should anyone bother?

Perhaps that customer wants to look good, look like his dad looked, or like Michael Jackson looked; it makes him feel good. More confident. More likely to contribute and feel empowered.

Perhaps it's for someone who likes the status of having someone wait on him. Once a week, he gets to sit in a throne, with a well-dressed, respectful craftsperson putting effort into his appearance.

Perhaps it's a signifier. That he wouldn't bother with this except it's what people like him are supposed to do. And not any shoeshine. *This* shoeshine, in this public spot, from this respected craftsperson.

Any of these edges and stories and transformations are available to the craftsperson as soon as he decides to make a difference.

Knowing that this is the story your customer tells himself is insufficient. You still have to act on it, open the door to the possibility, and organize the entire experience around that story.

This is the work that helps people understand that you are special, and this is the work that makes things better.

When you know what you stand for, you don't need to compete

Bernadette Jiwa has written half a dozen extraordinary books that humanize the too-often industrialized craft of marketing.

In *Story Driven*, she makes it clear that if we merely try to fill a hole in the market, we're doomed to a cycle of rearview-mirror behavior. We're nothing but a commodity in the making, always wary of our competition. We have no choice but to be driven by scarcity, focused on maintaining or perhaps slightly increasing our market share.

The alternative is to find and build and earn your story, the arc of the change you seek to produce. This is a generative posture, one based on possibility, not scarcity.

Now that you've chosen your audience, where do you want to take them?

Bernadette shares ten things that good stories do; if the story you're telling yourself (and others) doesn't do these things for you, you might need to dig deeper and find a better story, one that's more true and more effective. Good stories:

1. Connect us to our purpose and vision for our career or business.
2. Allow us to celebrate our strengths by remembering how we got from there to here.
3. Deepen our understanding of our unique value and what differentiates us in the marketplace.
4. Reinforce our core values.
5. Help us to act in alignment and make value-based decisions.
6. Encourage us to respond to customers instead of react to the marketplace.
7. Attract customers who want to support businesses that reflect or represent their values.
8. Build brand loyalty and give customers a story to tell.
9. Attract the kind of like-minded employees we want.

10. Help us to stay motivated and continue to do work we're proud of.

But your story is a hook

And you're on it.

Once you claim a story, once you commit to wanting to help people change, to take them on a journey from here to there—then you're on the hook.

On the hook to deliver.

On the hook for what happens next.

Is it any wonder we'd prefer to make average stuff for average people? If all you do is offer an alternative, that's a low-risk path. Take it or leave it.

On the other hand, great marketing is the generous and audacious work of saying, "I see a better alternative; come with me."

Case Study: Stack Overflow is better

If you're a programmer, you've visited Stack Overflow. It's a profitable company with more than 250 employees, dealing with millions of visits a week. If you have a question, it's probably already been answered on one of their forums.

Stack Overflow saves programmers time and effort, and it's also a passion project for thousands of the volunteers who contribute content.

How did its founder Joel Spolsky make better happen?

In the early years of the 2000s, there was a programming forum called Experts Exchange. Their model was simple and obvious: They hosted answers to common programming questions, and you had to pay to read them. A subscription cost three hundred dollars per year.

In order to build the business, they came at it from a place of scarcity. The questions were free to read, but the answers cost money.

To get traffic, they tricked the primitive Google robots that search the web by showing them the answers (which got them good search engine traffic), but when people showed up they scrambled the information, hiding the answers until people subscribed.

Experts Exchange created profit via frustration.

Joel worked with his cofounder, programmer Jeff Atwood, to come up with a different approach: make the questions visible, make the answers visible, and pay for the whole thing with job advertising. After all, what better place to find great programmers than a website where great programmers come to ask questions and give answers?

Along the way, Joel discovered that creating a better product meant treating different people differently, telling stories to each constituency that matched its worldview and needs.

For programmers in a hurry, he made it easy to find a question and the best answer for it. The answers are ranked by quality, so programmers don't waste time.

He realized that for every person who answered a question, a thousand people wanted an answer. Instead of trying to frustrate questioners, he got out of their way and gave them what they needed.

But answerers were different. For them, he built a community, a ranking system, a series of levels that would enable them to build a reputation and be rewarded with power over the community.

And job board posters were different as well. They wanted a fast, efficient, self-service method to find the best people. No hard sell, no distractions.

Joel didn't want to put his personal stamp on a personal site. He set out to be of service, to make things more efficient, to tell people a story that they wanted and needed to hear.

He built something better, and he let the core audience not only spread the word but do the thing that an outsider might have thought of as work.

Better is up to the users, not up to you

Google is better.

It was better than Bing and better than Yahoo!

Better in what way?

The search results weren't obviously better.

The search itself wasn't dramatically faster.

What was better was that the search box didn't make you feel stupid.

Yahoo! had 183 links on their home page. Google had two.

It projected confidence and clarity. You couldn't break it.

So it was better—for some people.

Now, DuckDuckGo is better. Because it isn't part of a big company. Because it doesn't track you. Because it's different.

So it's better—for some people.

"And we serve coffee"

Until a fire temporarily shut them down (actually, it was the sprinklers, not the coffeemaker, that did the damage), Trident Booksellers and Café in Boston was one of the most vibrant and successful bookstores in the country.

No matter how cheap and big Amazon got, Trident managed to do pretty well. Because they do something Amazon can't. *They serve coffee.*

If you run a retail store that competes with anyone online, ". . . and we serve coffee" is not a bad tagline.

That's because coffee is better together.

Coffee creates a third place: a spot to meet, to connect, to dream.

And so Trident is actually a coffee shop that sells books.

The books we just bought are a souvenir of the personal connections we made today.

The authentic, vulnerable hero

You know this archetype: the woman who shows up with her full self, her inner truth, ready to withstand the slings and arrows of a world that doesn't get her, until it does, and then they celebrate.

This is a myth.

It's a dangerous myth.

There are a few exceptions that prove the rule, but in general, what's true is that we need people willing to be of service.

Service to the change they seek to make.

Willing to tell a story that resonates with a group that they care enough to serve.

There could be an overlap. It's possible that it's the way you feel right this minute, but it might not be. The version of you on offer might run many layers deep, but it can't possibly be all of you, all the time.

A professional plays a role, doing the best possible work, regardless of the day or the patient or the client.

When James Brown fell on his knees on stage, exhausted, needing to be resuscitated by his attendants, it was brilliant stagecraft, not an authentic performance. After all, it happened every night.

When a therapist changes lives all day long by listening patiently, he actually might be patient, but it's more likely he's simply doing his job.

When the barista at Starbucks smiles at you and wishes you a great day, he's presenting, not revealing.

That's fine, because revealing isn't what better looks like. Revealing is reserved for your family and your closest friends, not the marketplace.

Protect yourself. You'll be needed tomorrow.

Service

Marketing acts (interesting choice of word, *acts*) are the generous actions of people who care. James Brown and the therapist understand that authenticity in the marketplace is a myth, that what people want is to be understood and to be served, not merely to witness whatever you feel like doing in a given moment.

And when we do the best version of our best work, our responsibility isn't to make it for ourselves . . . it's to bring it to the person we seek to serve. We reserve our best version of the work for them, not for us. Just as a three-star chef doesn't cook herself a twelve-course meal for dinner, you are not expected (or welcome) to bring us every one of your insecurities, innermost fears, and urgent demands.

You're here to serve.

Authenticity versus emotional labor

Emotional labor is the work of doing what we don't feel like doing. It's about showing up with a smile when we're wincing inside, or resisting the urge to chew someone out because you know that engaging with him will make a bigger difference.

It takes a small amount of energy and guts to be authentic. You need to feel confident enough to let your true feelings be exposed, knowing that if you're rejected, it's personal.

But there's a lot of hiding involved as well—hiding from the important work of making change happen. If all you do is follow your (make-believe) muse, you may discover that the muse is a chicken, and it's steering you away from the important work. And if the authentic you is a selfish jerk, please leave him at home.

If you need to be authentic to do your best work, you're not a professional, you're a fortunate amateur. Fortunate, because you have a gig where being the person you feel like being in the moment actually helps you move forward.

For the rest of us, there's the opportunity to be a professional, to exert emotional labor in search of empathy—the empathy to imagine what someone else would want, what they might believe, what story would resonate with them.

We don't do this work because we feel like it in the moment. We do this work, this draining emotional labor, because we're professionals, and because we want to make change happen.

Emotional labor is the work we do to provide service.

Who's talking?

When you get an email from a faceless corporation, speaking in the second person, someone is hiding. It's slick, but it's not real. We don't feel a connection, merely the shadow of a bureaucrat.

On the other hand, when a human being extends emotional labor to take responsibility—"Here, I made this"—then the door is open to connection and growth.

The most effective organizations don't always have a famous leader or a signature on every email. But they act like they do.

"Here, I made this."

The goal isn't to personalize the work. It's to make it personal.

CHAPTER SEVEN

The Canvas of Dreams and Desires

Everything you've been taught in school and at work about doing a good job has been about meeting spec, delivering on the assignment, getting the A, doing the specific thing for the specific industrial purpose.

"What do you do" is about a task, a measurable, buyable thing.

Consider this job description from the U.S. government:

SEWING MACHINE OPERATOR; GRADE: 6

Sets up and runs a variety of domestic and industrial type power operated sewing machines and related special purpose machines such as buttonhole, basting and feed-off the arm machines. . . .

Makes independent judgments and decisions within the framework of oral or written instructions and accepted methods, techniques, and procedures. Continually handles objects weighing up to 5 kilograms (10 pounds) and occasionally objects weighing up to 9 kilograms (20 pounds). Works inside in areas that usually have adequate light, heat and fresh air. Is exposed to the possibility of cuts and bruises.

While this is the description of a *job*, it's not the description of a dream or a desire. While it's specific, it could easily be changed without altering what it delivers.

This is how money works as well. Twenty-dollar bills are meaningless. It's what you can buy with them that we work for.

The same is true of your product or service. You may say you're offering a widget, but don't believe it. When you're marketing change, you're offering a new emotional state, a step closer to the dreams and desires of your customers, not a widget.

We sell feelings, status, and connection, not tasks or stuff.

What do people want?

If you ask them, you probably won't find what you're looking for. You certainly won't find a breakthrough. It's our job to watch people, figure out what they dream of, and then create a transaction that can deliver that feeling.

The crowd didn't invent the Model T, the smartphone, or rap. The crowd didn't invent JetBlue, City Bakery, or charity: water either.

Crowdfunding is one thing, but the crowd isn't that good at inventing a breakthrough.

There are three common confusions that many of us get stuck on.

The first is that *people confuse wants and needs*. What we

need is air, water, health, and a roof over our heads. Pretty much everything else is a want. And if we're privileged enough, we decide that those other things we want are actually needs.

The second is that people are intimately aware of their wants (which they think of as needs) but *they are absolutely terrible at inventing new ways to address those wants*. They often prefer to use a familiar solution to satisfy their wants, even if it's not working very well. When it comes time to innovate, they get stuck.

The third is *mistakenly believing that everyone wants the same thing*. In fact, we don't. The early adopters want things that are new; the laggards want things to never change. One part of the population wants chocolate, another vanilla.

Innovative marketers invent new solutions that work with old emotions

While the seven billion people on this planet are each unique, each a different collection of wants, needs, pain, and joy, in many ways we're all the same. We share a basket of dreams and desires, all in different proportions, but with a ton of overlap.

Here's the list, the foundational list, a shared vocabulary that each of us chooses from when expressing our dreams and fears:

Adventure	Belonging
Affection	Community
Avoiding new things	Control

Creativity	Physical activity
Delight	Power
Freedom of expression	Reassurance
Freedom of movement	Reliability
Friendship	Respect
Good looks	Revenge
Health	Romance
Learning new things	Safety
Luxury	Security
Nostalgia	Sex
Obedience	Strength
Participation	Sympathy
Peace of mind	Tension

You could probably add ten more. But it's unlikely you could add fifty more. This core basket of dreams and desires means that marketers, like artists, don't need many colors to paint an original masterpiece.

And this is where we begin: with assertions. Assertions about what our audience, the folks we need to serve, want and need. Assertions about what's on their minds when they wake up, what they talk about when no one is eavesdropping, what they remember at the end of the day.

And then we make assertions about how our story and our promise will interact with these wants and desires. When someone encounters us, will they see what we see? Will they want what we think they'll want? Will they take action?

Don't begin with your machines, your inventory, or your tactics. Don't begin with what you know how to do or some sort of distraction about your mission. Instead, begin with dreams and fears, with emotional states, and with the change your customers seek.

Nobody needs your product

It doesn't make sense to say "people need a white leather wallet," because:

1. People don't need a wallet. They might *want* one, but that's different.
2. People might decide that they want a white leather wallet, but they don't want it because it's white or because it's leather; they want it because of how it will make them feel. That's what they're buying: a feeling, not a wallet. Identify that feeling before you spend time making a wallet.

Marketers make change. We change people from one emotional state to another. We take people on a journey; we help them become the person they've dreamed of becoming, a little bit at a time.

No one is happy to call a real estate broker

Not really. Despite what the broker is hoping, this isn't often a joyous interaction.

They're afraid.

Nervous.

Relieved.

Eager to get going.

Anxious about moving.

Stressed about money.

Thinking about status gained or lost.

Concerned about the future.

Worried about their kids.

The broker is a speed bump on the way to their future. And most of what he or she says is merely noise, a palliative, because it all costs the same anyway.

According to statistics given to me by the National Association of Realtors, more than 80 percent of the people who hire a broker do so by choosing the first person to return their call.

Given that, here's what I'd ask a broker seeking *better*: How will you choose to show up in the world? Will you reassure and soothe? Will you probe and explore? Will you claim that you're better, faster, more caring?

Just as no one needs a drill bit, no one needs a real estate broker. What they need and want is how it makes them feel to get what a broker can get them.

(And the same thing is true for waiters, for limo drivers, and perhaps for you . . .)

Like real estate brokers, most of us do our most important work when we traffic in emotions, not commodities.

Where's the angry bear?

When someone doesn't act as you expected them to, look for their fear.

It's difficult to dream of anything when you think you're about to be eaten by a grizzly. Even (or especially) if it's all in your mind.

What do you want?

Let me guess. You'd like to be respected, successful, independent, appropriately busy, and maybe a little famous. You'd like to do work you're proud of and do it for people you care about.

What's not on that list? That you need to own a certain color car. That you have to sell your items in packages that are six inches wide, not seven inches. That you want all your customers to have first names with no fewer than six letters in them.

The details don't matter so much. Just as your customers want a shift in their emotional states, to move from fear to belonging, so do you.

That leaves a huge amount of room. Many degrees of freedom.

It helps to follow certain truths of commerce. If you want to be independent, you probably need to own assets, or a reputation. If you want to be financially well off, you probably need to deliver enough value to the right people that they will happily pay you for it. If you want to be proud of your work, you probably need to avoid racing to the bottom and denigrating the culture along the way.

Within that framework, though, there's plenty of room. Room for you to dig in deep and decide what change you want to make, and how (and who) you seek to serve.

This might be a good time to go back to the edges exercise, to go through it again and find some new axes, new revelations, new promises. Find the people worth serving, and then find a change worth making.

Always be testing

It's tempting to make a boring product or service for everyone.

Boring because boring is beyond criticism. It meets spec. It causes no tension.

Everyone, because if everyone is happy then no one is unhappy.

The problem is that the marketplace of people who are happy with boring is static. They aren't looking for better.

New and boring don't easily coexist, and so the people who are happy with boring aren't looking for you. They're actively avoiding you, in fact.

The ever-faster cycles that require us to always be testing, to resist creating boredom, are driven by the fact that the only people we can serve are curious, dissatisfied, or bored. Everyone else can opt out and refuse to pay attention.

The good news is that two extraordinary things have happened, massive shifts in the way everything is sold to everyone:

1. It's cheaper and faster than ever to create a prototype or a limited run. That's true for nonprofits, as well as for manufacturers or service businesses.
2. It's cheaper and faster than ever to find the early adopters, to engage with people who want to hear from you.

This means it's on each of us to make an assertion. Outline a promise. Choose your extremes, find the people you seek to change, and show up with your offer.

Call it a test if you want to.

But it's real life.

The real life of engaging with what's possible, and of working with people who want to make a change.

Always be seeking, connecting, solving, asserting, believing, seeing, and yes, testing.

The other way to read this is: *always be wrong.*

Well, not always. Sometimes you'll be right. But most of the time, you'll be wrong. That's okay.

Scrapbooking

Being wrong from scratch is exhausting. Radical originality doesn't have a high return on investment, and it will wear you out.

Scrapbooking is an efficient alternative.

When designing a website, or an email campaign, or a new product, you can scrapbook it.

Find the things you think that those you engage with will be attracted to and will trust. The typefaces, the pricing, the offers, the images, the interfaces . . . and cut them up, break them down into the original indivisible memes within. Then rebuild something new on top of these pieces.

You can do the same thing when you put together your website, your podcast, or your new project. Find the essential beacons (the extremes) that matter to you and to your audience, and weave them together in a new thing.

If you had to charge ten times as much

What's the difference between a thirty-dollar massage and a three hundred-dollar one?

What could make a book worth two hundred dollars? Or a hotel room worth fifteen hundred dollars? What could cause someone to give five hundred dollars to charity instead of fifty dollars?

"More of the same" is the wrong answer.

In order to dramatically increase the size of your audience or the price that you charge, you'll need to do more than simply work more hours or interrupt more people.

We don't pay ten times extra for more words, a bigger order of French fries, or a louder stereo.

Instead, it's a different extreme, a different story, a different sort of scarcity.

Irresistible is rarely easy or rational

There's often a line out the door of Fiona's shop.

It's not surprising. The ice cream is delicious, the portions are enormous, and a waffle cone costs less than three Canadian dollars. And it's served with a smile, almost a grin.

It's irresistible.

Of course, once you finish the cone, you'll stroll around, hang out by the water, and maybe start to make plans about where to spend a week of next year's vacation.

The Opinicon, a lovely little resort near Ottawa, could charge a lot more for an ice cream cone. A team of MBAs doing a market analysis and a profit and loss report would probably pin the value at about eight dollars. That's where the return on investment would be at its peak.

But they're not in the business of selling ice cream cones. *The ice cream cones are a symbol, a beacon, a chance to engage.*

If you run everything through a spreadsheet, you might end up with a rational plan, but the rational plan isn't what creates energy or magic or memories.

Stew Leonard's was a small supermarket with a big footprint. It was profiled by Tom Peters and had the highest sales per square foot of any store of its kind. Stew's was an experience, almost an amusement park, with remarkable customer service, clever merchandising, and interesting products to choose from. As the company grew to a few more stores, a new generation of owners took over who seemed more intent on short-term profit and less focused on magic. For a while, profits increased. But now, year after year, it's a bit less crowded, a bit less energetic, a bit less interesting. So when a new store opens nearby, they lose a few more customers, then a few more, and finally, people begin to wonder, "Why do I even bother coming here in the first place?"

It might not be about being cheaper. It's tricky to define better. But without a doubt, the heart and soul of a thriving enterprise is the irrational pursuit of becoming irresistible.

CHAPTER EIGHT

More of the Who: Seeking the Smallest Viable Market

The virtuous cycle and network effects

Every very good customer gets you another one.

Dead-end customers aren't worth the trouble. Silent customers, jealous customers, people who think you need to be kept a secret . . . you can't grow your work on a cul de sac.

Your best customers become your new salespeople.

Your work to change the culture thrives when the word spreads, and if you want the word to spread, you need to build something that works better when it gets spread.

That creates the positive cycle you're seeking. The one that makes change happen.

The most effective remarkability comes from design

The fax machine was remarkable. It spread not because of a clever ad campaign, but because users chose to talk about it.

Why?

Because the fax machine works better if your colleagues have one too.

Bob Metcalfe saw this firsthand when he invented Ethernet. 3Com's original offering permitted three users to hook up their PCs and share a printer. That's a marginal benefit, not much to talk about.

But once users began to share data, everything changed. Now, you were in one of two states: in the network or off the network. And if you were isolated, off the network, that was painful. The more people joined the network, the more people talked about the network. That made isolation even more painful.

The original slide behind Metcalfe's Law had just two lines on it. The straight line shows that the cost of adding each person to the network goes up slowly. The curved line, though, shows that the value of adding one more person to the network is exponentially greater.

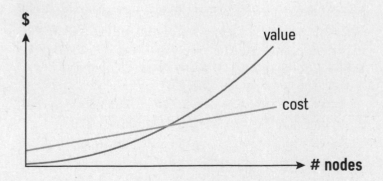

This simple network effect is at the heart of every mass movement and every successful culture change. It happens when remarkable is designed right into the story of your change, and more important, when the product or service works better when I use it with others.

The conversation I'm motivated to have with my peers becomes the engine of growth. Growth creates more value, which leads to more growth.

"And then a miracle happens"

Here's the truth about customer traction: a miracle isn't going to happen.

The old-school marketer's dream revolves around transforming a product, this normal, average, "it's fine" product or service . . . the one that's sitting there, with nothing much happening. Transform it into a hit.

The dream is that with public relations, with hype, with promotion, with distribution, with ad buys, with influence marketing, with content marketing, and with a little bit of spam . . . the dream is that it will become the "it" thing, and everyone will want it. It will be popular precisely because it's popular.

But you're not fooled by this.

Sure, every so often a superstar is born, but most of the time, this approach merely leads to failure. Expensive failure.

The alternative is to seek a path, not a miracle.

And that path begins with customer traction.

Here's what I want to know about your VC–backed Silicon Valley startup: How many people outside of HQ use it every day? How often are they sending you suggestions to make it better?

Here's what else I want to know: How many people are insisting that their friends and colleagues use it? As in *right now.*

Do they love it? Do they love themselves more because they love you?

That restaurant you just opened: How many people come back night after night to eat there, bringing new friends each time?

Or that booth at the farmers' market, or the nonprofit you're starting, or your local babysitting service.

Who would miss it if it were gone?

If you can't succeed in the small, why do you believe you will succeed in the large?

A thousand true fans

In 2008 Kevin Kelly, founding editor of *Wired,* wrote an essay that described the simple truth of the smallest viable market.

For the independent creator of intellectual property (a singer, perhaps, or a writer), it turns out that a thousand true fans might be sufficient to live a better-than-decent life.

To quote Kevin, "A true fan is defined as a fan that will buy anything you produce. These diehard fans will drive two hundred miles to see you sing; they will buy the hardback and paperback and Audible versions of your book; they will purchase your next figurine sight unseen; they will pay for the 'best-of'

DVD version of your free YouTube channel; they will come to your chef's table once a month. If you have roughly a thousand true fans like this (also known as super fans), you can make a living—if you are content to make a living but not a fortune."

That's one thousand people who will support you on Patreon, or one thousand people who will buy your new project on Kickstarter the day you launch it. It's one thousand people who not only care about your work but also spread the word to those around them.

The challenge for most people who seek to make an impact isn't winning over the mass market. It's the micro market. They bend themselves into a pretzel trying to please the anonymous masses before they have fifty or one hundred people who would miss them if they were gone.

While it might be comforting to dream of becoming a Kardashian, it's way more productive to matter to a few instead.

But what about *Hamilton*?

The hit that proves the theory. The hit that represents not only the triumph of one creator over the status quo, but the magical narrative of a singular piece of effort and art that changes everything.

Except.

Except, for more than a year, *Hamilton* was seen by only a few hundred people a night.

Except that even when it is running at full capacity in New

York, breaking records on Broadway, it's only being seen by a few thousand people.

Except that even as it's changing a small part of the culture in cities like Chicago, it has been seen by less than 1 percent of the U.S. population. Its best-selling soundtrack album only sold a few hundred thousand copies. And the companion book, a surprise best-seller, sold about that many as well.

Our hits aren't hits anymore, not like they used to be. Instead, they are meaningful for a few and invisible to the rest.

What would Jerry do?

I often tell the story of the Grateful Dead, and yet almost no one has the guts to commit to this sort of service, the leadership of connection. I first wrote about them ten years ago, and yet too many of us fall into the trap of seeking whatever passes for the Top 40 in our industry instead.

So far I've purchased 233 different Grateful Dead albums, more than five hundred hours of music altogether.

The Dead are an almost perfect example of the power of marketing for the smallest viable market. It's worth a few minutes to deconstruct what they did and how they did it, because it will inform the long, strange trip we're on here.

Although it's become a familiar example, musicians, publishers, gym owners, consultants, chefs, and teachers seem to forget the core lesson in the Dead's failure to race for a hit.

First, few kids grow up wanting to start a band like the

Grateful Dead. The Dead had a grand total of one top 40 Billboard hit. *One*.

They're easily dismissed as some sort of quirky hippie band. They have fans, true fans, fans who are also easily dismissed as quirky hippies.

And yet . . .

And yet the Dead grossed more than $350 million in revenue while Jerry Garcia was alive, and another $100 million since his death. I'm not even counting record sales, just concert tickets. Most of that run was accomplished when ticket prices averaged just twenty-three dollars.

How? Because the true fans showed up. Because the true fans spread the word. And because the true fans never fully satisfied their need to be connected.

Here are the key elements of the Dead's marketing success:

- They appealed to a relatively tiny audience and focused all their energy on them.

- They didn't use radio to spread their ideas to the masses. Instead, they relied on fans to share the word, hand to hand, by encouraging them to tape their shows.

- Instead of hoping to encourage a large number of people to support them a little, they relied on a small number of true fans who supported them a lot.

- They picked the extremes on the XY axis (live concerts vs. polished records, long jams for the fan family vs. short hits for the radio) and owned them both.

- They gave the fans plenty to talk about and stand for. Insiders and outsiders.

They needed three things to pull this off:

- Extraordinary talent. You can't fake your way through 146 concerts in a year.

- Significant patience. In 1972, considered by some to be a peak year for the band, only five thousand people came to a typical show. It took more than a decade before the Dead became an "overnight" success.

- The guts to be quirky. It couldn't have been easy to watch the Zombies, the Doors, and even the Turtles sell far more records than they did. For a while, anyway.

In 1972, being obstinate, generous, and lucky was an accident that led to their surprising success. Today, though, in most industries (including the music business) this sort of success is not an accident. It's the best path to success, and in many ways, the most rewarding as well.

Taylor Swift is not your role model

Consider Scott Borchetta, who runs Big Machine records. He's had more than *two hundred* number-one singles. That's an awe-inspiring total. A world-class marketer.

He's sold more than thirty million records for Taylor Swift, and Swift's tour revenue is about the same as the Dead's was.

Taylor and Scott are hit machines.

Most markets need someone to be a hit machine, and for the music business right now, it's them. As we'll see, every long tail has a short head, a place where the hits live. Hits serve a useful purpose to our culture, but the essential lesson is this: someone is going to make hits, and it's probably not going to be you.

If you can find a playbook on how to become a hit machine, to become the one who regularly creates the mass movement that changes the middle of the market, go for it!

For the rest of us, there's the other path: the path of connection, empathy, and change.

All critics are right (all critics are wrong)

The critic who doesn't like your work is correct. He doesn't like your work. This cannot be argued with.

The critic who says that no one else will like your work is wrong. After all, you like your work. Someone else might like it too.

This is the only way to understand the one-star and five-star reviews that every bestselling book on Amazon receives. How could one book possibly get both? Either it's good or it's not.

Not true.

Twelve percent of the twenty-one thousand reviews for *Harry Potter and the Sorcerer's Stone* gave it one or two stars. To visualize that: out of one hundred readers, twelve said it was one of the worst books they'd ever read.

What this bimodal distribution teaches us is that there are at least two audiences that interact with every bestselling book.

There's the desired audience, the one that has a set of dreams and beliefs and wants that perfectly integrates with this work. And there's the accidental audience, the one that gets more satisfaction out of not liking the work, out of hating it, and sharing that thought with others.

They're both right.

But neither is particularly useful.

When we seek feedback, we're doing something brave and foolish. We're asking to be proven wrong. To have people say "You thought you made something great, but you didn't."

Ouch.

What if, instead, we seek advice?

Seek it like this: "I made something that I like, that I thought you'd like. How'd I do? What advice do you have for how I could make it fit your worldview more closely?"

That's not criticism. Or feedback. That sort of helpful advice reveals a lot about the person you're engaging with. It helps us see his or her fears and dreams and wants. It's a clue on how to get even closer next time.

Plenty of people can tell you how your work makes them feel. We're intimately familiar with the noise in our own heads, and that noise is often expressed as personal and specific criticism.

But it might not be about you and it might not be useful.

Perhaps you're hearing about someone's fears, or their narrative about inadequacy or unfairness.

When people share their negative stories, they often try to

broaden the response and universalize it. They talk about how "no one" or "everyone" will feel. But what you're actually hearing about is a specific sore spot that was touched in a specific moment by a specific piece of work.

This is the person who posts a one-star review because the book arrived late for the baby shower. Or the customer who's angry because she spent more than she budgeted for on her wedding. That's quite different from someone giving you useful advice about how to work with someone like them in the future.

It's worth the effort to insulate ourselves from a raw emotional onslaught and to tease out substantial useful direction instead.

Why don't people choose you?

Here's another difficult exercise, one that stretches the empathy muscle of a typical marketer:

Those people who don't buy from you, the ones who don't take your calls, who sneer at your innovations, who happily buy from a competitor even if they know you exist . . . *those* people . . .

Why are they right?

Why are the people who don't choose you correct in their decision to not choose you?

If you've worked hard, it's tempting to denigrate their judgment, to question their values, and assume that these folks are either ill-informed, selfish, or simply wrongheaded.

Put that aside for a moment and find the empathy to fill in this sentence: "For people who want what you want (_____) and believe what you believe (_____), your choice of _____ is exactly correct."

Because it is.

People are quite likely to make perfectly rational decisions based on what they see, what they believe, and what they want.

If you're a career coach, then explain why people who don't hire a coach have made a smart decision. Or explain why people who are using someone else to coach them have done something that makes sense for them.

Years ago, I went to a cooking class that a friend had bought me as a gift. The chef was teaching everyone to make a dish that used ground veal. "Any questions?" he asked. One student had the temerity to raise his hand and ask, "Is it okay to make this dish with ground turkey instead?"

In a thick accent, the chef sneered, "You could . . . if you wanted it to taste like *dirt*."

Of course, they were both right.

For the student, the availability, health benefits, or moral imperatives associated with choosing turkey over veal might mean that he cared more about the story than he did about matching the taste profile that was on offer. For the teacher, for whom the Proustian memory of this dish was everything, the idea of substitutions disrespected the effort he was putting into his work.

That's what right means in this case. Based on who they are

and what they want and what they know, everyone is right. Every time.

When we find the empathy to say, "I'm sorry, this isn't for you, here's the phone number of my competitor," then we also find the freedom to do work that matters.

CHAPTER NINE

People Like Us Do Things Like This

Deep change is difficult, and worth it

As we've seen, every organization, every project, every interaction exists to do one thing: to make change happen.

To make a sale, to change a policy, to heal the world.

As marketers and agents of change, we almost always overrate our ability to make change happen. The reason is simple.

Everyone always acts in accordance with their internal narratives.

You can't get someone to do something that they don't want to do, and most of the time, what people want to do is take action (or not take action) that reinforces their internal narratives.

The real question, then, is where does the internal narrative come from, and how does *it* get changed? Or, more likely, how do we use the internal narrative to change the actions that people take?

Some people have an internal narrative that makes them open to changing their behavior (e.g., Quincy Jones likes many kinds of music), while others begin the process with great resistance.

For most of us, though, changing our behavior is driven by our *desire to fit in* (people like us do things like this) and our *perception of our status* (affiliation and dominance). Since both these forces often push us to stay as we are, it takes tension to change them.

Once you see these forces at work, you'll be able to navigate the culture in a whole new way. It will be as if someone turned on the lights and gave you a map.

People like us (do things like this)

Have you eaten crickets? Never mind the crunchy insect-shaped kind, but even cricket flour? In many parts of the world, crickets are a fine source of protein.

What about beef? Even though this is one of the most easily addressed causes of global warming, even though beef is a truly inefficient way to feed the world, it's safe to say that most people reading this have had beef for lunch or dinner sometime in the last week.

If it's not genetic, if we're not born with a predetermined feeling about crickets versus beef, if there are no clear-cut rational reasons to eat one or the other, why do crickets make us squirm while cows make us hungry (or vice versa)?

Because people like us eat things like this.

For most of us, from the first day we are able to remember

until the last day we breathe, our actions are primarily driven by one question: "Do people like me do things like this?"

People like me don't cheat on their taxes.

People like me own a car; we don't take the bus.

People like me have a full-time job.

People like me want to see the new James Bond movie.

Even when we adopt the behavior of an outlier, when we do something the crowd doesn't often do, we're still aligning ourselves with the behavior of outliers.

Nobody is unaware and uncaring of what is going on around him. No one who is wholly original, self-directed, and isolated in every way. A sociopath might do things in opposition to the crowd, but he's not unaware of the crowd.

We can't change *the* culture, but each of us has the opportunity to change a culture—our little pocket of the world.

The smallest viable market makes sense because it maximizes your chances of changing a culture. The core of your market, enriched and connected by the change you seek to make, organically shares the word with the next layer of the market. And so on. This is *people like us*.

Case Study: The Blue Ribbons

My little town had a problem. Despite having extraordinary schools (our elementary school had won the national Blue Ribbon School designation), there was a schism over the upcoming budget vote.

Many in town, particularly longtime residents and second- or third-generation families, were upset about rising school taxes. Some of them organized and, for the first time in memory, the school budget vote failed.

In New York state, the school gets a second vote, but if that fails as well, the mandated cuts are quite draconian, with essential programs cut without thoughtful prioritization. With only eight days before the next vote, what could be done?

A few activists decided to try a new approach. Instead of arguing vociferously in favor of the budget, instead of passing out flyers or holding a rally, they tied one hundred blue ribbons to a big tree in front of the middle school, right in the center of town.

Within days, the idea had spread. In the week before the election, many dozens of trees, all around town, had blue ribbons hanging from them. Thousands of blue ribbons, hung by dozens of families.

The message was simple—people like us, people in our town, people in this Blue Ribbon district, support our schools.

The budget passed two to one.

The internal narrative

We don't make decisions in a vacuum—instead, we base them on our perception of our cohort. So we buy a $700 baby stroller because we're smart (or we don't, because it's stupid).

Or we shop at the local farmers' market (or we don't, because it's raining, and they don't sell Cheetos).

We harass the female TV reporter outside the soccer stadium (and lose our jobs) because that's how we see our people behaving.

Or we wear a bright pink shirt, yellow trousers, and no socks, because, we tell ourselves, they're comfortable (but mostly it's because that's how we imagine a successful version of ourselves.)

It's all built around the simple question: "Do people like me do things like this?"

Normalization creates culture, and culture drives our choices, which leads to more normalization.

Marketers don't make average stuff for average people. Marketers make change. And they do it by normalizing new behaviors.

Defining "us"

In the previous era, mass media worked hard to define "us" as "all of us," as the crowd, the Americans, the people of the world. All of us never totally succeeded, because the racists and the xenophobes and the isolated were happy to draw the line somewhere short of all of us.

It got very close, though. "I'd like to teach the world to sing" and the commercialization of the entire world happened faster and more deeply than most people expected. We (mostly) all watched Johnny Carson and we (mostly) all wore jeans and we (mostly) all went to school. At least the *all* that stretched as far as we were willing to see.

Today, though, popular culture isn't as popular as it used to be. *Mad Men*, which was hyped by the *New York Times* in dozens of articles in just one season, was only regularly seen by 1 percent of the U.S. population. And the popular culture phenomenon that is the Cronut, or the deep-fried Oreo at the county fair, or the raw moon pie at the funky restaurant—these phenomena reach, if you're willing to do a little rounding, basically no one.

We've gone from all of us being *everyone* to all of us being *no one*.

But that's okay, because the long tail of culture and the media and change doesn't need everyone any longer. It's happy with *enough*.

Which us?

In "People like us do things like this," the "us" matters. The more specific, the more connected, the tighter the "us," the better.

What the marketer, the leader, and the organizer must do as their first job is simple: define "us."

When you say "People like us donate to a charity like this one," you're clearly not saying it to everyone. Everyone is not going to give to your charity. So, who is?

The right answer is *not* "The people who give are people like us." That's backwards. We need to be braver than that, more articulate, more willing to take initiative in not only reaching our markets but changing them, changing their expectations, and most of all, changing what they choose to tell and show each other.

The same calculus applies in the internal meeting where

you're pitching a new idea to your company, or the business-to-business sales call you're making, or the way you hope to shift the culture of the soccer team you coach.

Begin with us.

It shouldn't be called "the culture"

It should be called "a culture" or "this culture," because there is no universal culture, no "us" that defines all of us.

When we're comfortable realizing that our work is to change "a culture," then we can begin to do two bits of hard work:

1. Map and understand the worldview of the culture we seek to change.
2. Focus all our energy on this group. Ignore everyone else. Instead, focus on building and living a story that will resonate with the culture we are seeking to change.

That's how we make change—by caring enough to want to change a culture, and by being brave enough to pick just one.

Just enough art

Entrepreneur Alex Samuel points out that when JetBlue launched, it simply had to be hipper than American and Delta.

But when Virgin America launched six years later, it had to be hipper than JetBlue. That's a different hurdle. After all, Jet-Blue had worked hard to be hip. The bar had been raised.

Everything in our culture is part of a hierarchy between yesterday, today, and tomorrow. We don't get to jump all the way ahead.

Photography works this way, for example. It's quite easy to be the photographer who is skilled enough to take yesterday's pictures. Previous styles are technically easy to mimic. That's straightforward. But to be the one who establishes the next phase takes a leap. A leap into a new way of doing something, just a bit better and a bit unexpected. Leap too far, though, and the tribe won't follow.

Case Study: Gay marriage in Ireland

One way to pass the world's first national referendum about the right for gay people to marry would be to state your case, to focus on fairness, respect, and civil rights.

That rational approach won't get you very far, though.

An alternative? Brighid White and her husband, Paddy, both nearly eighty, made a video about their son and about what it meant to them to support the referendum.

People like us.

It's easy for some to watch that video and see themselves. As parents. As traditionalists. As Irishmen.

The essence of political change is almost always cultural change, and the culture changes horizontally.

Person to person. Us to us.

Elite and/or exclusive

Malcolm Gladwell pointed out that there's a difference between an elite institution and an exclusive one.

They can coexist, but often don't.

The Rhodes Scholarship is an elite award. It goes to few people, and it's respected by other elite individuals and institutions.

Elite is an external measure. Does the world you care about respect this badge?

But the Rhodes Scholarship isn't exclusive. It's not a tribe, a group of well-connected individuals with their own culture.

Exclusive is an internal measure. It's us versus them, insiders versus outsiders.

The Hell's Angels aren't elite, but they're exclusive.

Harvard Business School is both elite and exclusive. So are the Navy Seals.

It's easy to get confused in our quest to build something that matters. It seems as though we ought to work to make our organization elite, to let the *New York Times* proclaim that our opera is worth seeing, or to hope that the upperclassmen will like our performance on the field.

In fact, though, it's exclusive institutions that change things. We have no control over our elite status, and it can be taken away in an instant. But exclusive organizations thrive as long as their members wish to belong, and that work is something we can control.

At the heart of the exclusive organization is a simple truth:

every member is "people like us." Sign up for that and you gain status. Walk away and you lose it.

In order to change a culture, we begin with an exclusive cohort. That's where we can offer the most tension and create the most useful connections.

Case Study: Robin Hood Foundation

In 2015, the Robin Hood Foundation raised $101,000,000.

In one night. It was the single most effective fundraiser of its kind in history.

Some people look at this result and conclude that the tactic (a gala) is the secret. It's not. It's the extraordinary peer pressure of *people like us do things like this.*

Robin Hood is a New York charity, supported largely by donations from wealthy hedge fund and Wall Street investors. The foundation had spent a generation building expectations about this event, carefully spreading the word about the generosity of the early adopters while playing into the hyper-competitive egomania of Wall Street. While there were a few anonymous gifts, almost all the money raised revolved around a simple trade: cash for status.

Tension is created by the event. You're there, your peers are there, your spouse is there. An auction is taking place. The cause is a good one. With a simple act, you can raise your profile, earn respect, and dominate the competition. If that matches your worldview and you believe you can afford it, then money is raised.

Over the years, this narrative is normalized. It's not extreme, not for this "us." Instead, it's what we do.

The intentional nature of this process is easily overlooked. It rarely happens as an unintentional side effect.

The standing ovation

How many people are needed to start a standing ovation?

At TED, it only takes three. If Bill and Al and Sunny leap to their feet, thousands of others will as well.

At a Broadway show, no matter how tepid the response, fifteen strangers spread throughout the theater might be enough.

And at Mezzrow, the awesome jazz club, it's probably not possible.

So, what's going on?

In some audiences, there are few strangers. We recognize and respect those around us, and our trust of these people, together with our deeply felt need to fit in, combine to activate a standing ovation. If I desire to be one of "us" and the leader is standing, well, I'll stand too.

On the other hand, in a venue of strangers, our desire to fit in is a bit different. At the Broadway theater, I'm wearing the tourist hat, and tourists like me respond in ways like this. The venue has a bias.

And the opposite is true among the hardcore jazz fans. They know that jazz fans don't give standing ovations, not in a club, and the bias of the venue is difficult to change.

Roots and shoots

Here's an analogy that helps bring to life the ideas we've covered so far:

Your work is a tree. The roots live in the soil of dreams and desires. Not the dreams and desires of *everyone*, simply those you seek to serve.

If your work is simply a commodity, a quick response to an obvious demand, then your roots don't run deep. It's unlikely that your tree will grow, or even if it does, it's unlikely to be seen as important, useful, or dominant. It will be crowded out by all the similar trees.

As your tree grows, it creates a beacon for the community. The early adopters among the people you seek to serve can engage with the tree, climb it, use it for shade, and, eventually, eat the fruits. And they attract the others.

If you have planned well, the tree will quickly grow taller, because the sun isn't being blocked—there are few other trees in the same area. As the tree grows, it not only attracts other people, but its height (as the dominant choice in the neighborhood) blocks out the futile efforts of other, similar trees. The market likes a winner.

It's a mistake to show up with an acorn and expect a crowd. Work that matters for people who care is the shortest, most direct route to making a difference.

CHAPTER TEN

Trust and Tension Create Forward Motion

Pattern match/pattern interrupt

You're going to do one or the other.

The pattern match is business as usual. When the offering you bring matches the story we tell ourselves, the way we tell it, the pace we're used to, the expense and the risk . . . it's an easy choice to add you to the mix.

Consider the family with young kids that's used to a never-ending parade of breakfast cereals. Cocoa Krispies led to Lucky Charms led to Frosted Flakes—whichever one is on sale or has a cool promo (that a kid yells about). When your new brand of cereal shows up, buying it is a pattern match. Sure, why not?

Or it might be as simple as a sitcom on Thursday night at 9 p.m. Millions sit down every week to watch TV . . . you're not trying to change their pattern; you're simply putting your new offering into the mix that already exists.

A pattern interrupt, on the other hand, requires some sort of jolt. Tension is created, and energy is diverted to consider this new input. Is it something worth considering? Most of the time, for most of those you seek to reach, the answer is no. The answer is no because the patterns are established, time is precious, and risk is something to be feared.

If you want someone who has never hired a gardener to hire you to be their gardener, you're asking for a pattern interrupt. If you are trying to secure a five thousand-dollar donation from a wealthy person who habitually makes hundred-dollar donations to charity, you face the same challenge. The pattern requires undoing before you can earn forward motion.

When life interferes, new patterns are established. This is why it's so profitable to market to new dads, engaged women, and people who have recently moved. They don't have a pattern to match, so it's *all* an interrupt. On the other hand, the purchasing manager at a typical organization has been taught that matching the pattern is the best way to keep a steady job with no surprises.

The best time to market a new app is when the platform is brand new.

When you market to someone who doesn't have a pattern yet, you don't have to persuade them that their old choices were mistakes.

Tension can change patterns

If you're going to market a pattern interrupt, it will require you to provide the kind of tension that can only be released by being willing to change an ingrained pattern.

Tension is the force on a stretched rubber band. Pull it at one end and it creates tension at every point.

Why do some people hesitate to ask a question during a class, but will happily answer the professor if they're called on?

Volunteering is a problem for them, because it requires agency and responsibility. But when the teacher applies focused social tension in the form of publicly calling on a student, that student has no problem answering. The tension was sufficient to overcome his or her inertia.

We create tension when we ask someone to contribute to the bake sale or join our book club. We're using one force (in this case, social engagement) to overcome another force (the status quo).

For an example, let's consider Slack, the fast-growing productivity software designed for teams at work. Very few people have a pattern of changing the way they work all day. No one wakes up in the morning hoping that they'll need to learn a new software program and deal with the hassle for weeks as they shift from a trusted platform to a new one.

And yet Slack is the fastest-growing product of its kind. How?

Because after capturing the energy and affection of some neophiliacs, the ratchet kicked in. Using Slack is better when your coworkers use it. So, existing users have a powerful selfish reason to tell the others, and in fact, every day they don't is painful for them.

And what about the pattern interrupt for the new user? Where's the tension?

Simple: a colleague says, "You're missing out."

Every day you're not on Slack, people at work are talking

about you behind your back, working on projects without you, having conversations you're excluded from.

You can release that tension, right now, simply by signing in . . .

Slack began by doing a *pattern match*, offering new software to people who like new software. A new way of doing work for people looking for a new way of doing work.

But then came the leap.

They gave this group a tool to create a *pattern interrupt*. Peer to peer. One worker saying to another, "We're going to try this new tool." That single horizontal transmission built a multi-billion-dollar software company.

It's not accidental. It's built into the software itself.

What pattern are you interrupting?

What are you breaking?

Launch a new project and, in addition to serving your audience, you'll be breaking something. The very existence of an alternative causes something else to no longer be true.

When you launch the second hotel in Niagara Falls, the first hotel is no longer the one and only.

When you launch the telephone, the telegraph is no longer the fastest way to send a message.

When you host an exclusive party, the people who aren't invited become outsiders.

When you launch an extreme (the most efficient, the least

expensive, the most convenient), then whatever you've exceeded is no longer the extreme that its fans sought out.

When a new network begins to gain traction, bringing in the cool kids, the powerful early adopters, this traction causes everyone who was part of the old network you're supplanting to reconsider their allegiance.

This is what tension feels like. The tension of being left behind.

And marketers who cause change cause tension.

Tension is not the same as fear

If you feel like you're coercing people, manipulating them or causing them to be afraid, you're probably doing it wrong.

But tension is different. Tension is something we can do precisely because we care about those we seek to serve.

Fear's a dream killer. It puts people into suspended animation, holding their breath, paralyzed and unable to move forward.

Fear alone isn't going to help you make change happen. Tension might, though.

The tension we face any time we're about to cross a threshold. The tension of this might work versus this might not work. The tension of, "If I learn this, will I like who I become?"

There might be fear, but tension is the promise that we can get through that fear to the other side.

Tension is the hallmark of a great educational experience— the tension of not quite knowing where we are in the process, not being sure of the curriculum, not having a guarantee that the insight we seek is about to happen.

All effective education creates tension, because just before you learn something, you're aware you don't know it (yet).

As adults, we willingly expose ourselves to the tension of a great jazz concert, or a baseball game, or a thrilling movie. But, mostly because we've been indoctrinated by fear, we hesitate when we have the opportunity to learn something new on our way to becoming the person we seek to be.

Fear will paralyze us if we haven't been taught that forward motion is possible. Once we see a way out, the tension can be the tool that moves us.

Effective marketers have the courage to create tension. Some actively seek out this tension, because it works. It pushes those you serve over the chasm to the other side.

If you care enough about the change you seek to make, you will care enough to generously and respectfully create tension on behalf of that change.

Marketers create tension, and forward motion relieves that tension

The logic of the going-out-of-business sale is elusive. After all, if the store was any good, it wouldn't be going out of business. And if a customer is hoping for support, a warranty, or a chance for a return, buying something from a store that's about to disappear isn't very smart.

And yet, people can't resist a bargain.

That's because the scarcity of the going-out-of-business sale creates tension. The tension of "What bargains did I miss?" The best way to relieve that tension is to go to the store and check it out.

Of course, the fear of missing out on a bankruptcy isn't the only tension that drives us forward.

Here's a new social app. If you get in early, you'll find more friends and be more in sync than the people who come later. Better not fall behind.

Here's how we process the invoices here. I know you're familiar with the original system, but our organization uses the new one, and you'll need to be good at it by Thursday.

The last three houses that sold on our block went for less than anyone expected. If we don't sell soon, we'll never be able to cover our mortgage.

Supreme is only making 250 of these sneakers. I'm getting a pair—are you coming?

If you want to find out how the series ends, you'll need to tune in on Sunday.

We don't want to feel left out, left behind, uninformed, or impotent. We want to get ahead. We want to be in sync. We want to do what people like us are doing.

None of those feelings existed before a marketer showed up with something that caused them—if there weren't a new album, you wouldn't feel left out if you hadn't heard it yet.

We intentionally create these gaps, these little canyons of tension that people find themselves leaping over.

And the reason is status.

Where do we stand?

What does the tribe think of us?

Who's up, and who's down?

Are you ready to create tension?

It's not a rhetorical question.

There are two ways to do your work.

You can be a cab driver. Show up and ask someone where they want to go. Charge them based on the meter. Be a replaceable cog in the on-demand transport system. You might be a harder-working cabbie, but it won't change much.

Or you can be an agent of change, someone who creates tension and then relieves it.

When they started building fancy casinos in Las Vegas, it created tension for countless travelers. Visitors who just a year earlier were happy in Reno or in downtown Las Vegas now felt like second-class citizens. They asked, "Am I the sort of person who goes to a casino this run-down?" The very existence of a fancier alternative degraded their experience at their former favorite.

Tension is created. And the only way to relieve that tension is with forward motion.

When you arrive on the scene with your story, with the solution you have in mind, do you also create tension? If you don't, the status quo is likely to survive.

How the status quo got that way

The dominant narrative, the market share leader, the policies and procedures that rule the day—they all exist for a reason.

They're good at resisting efforts by insurgents like you.

If all it took to upend the status quo was the truth, we would have changed a long time ago.

If all we were waiting for was a better idea, a simpler solution, or a more efficient procedure, we would have shifted away from the status quo a year or a decade or a century ago.

The status quo doesn't shift because you're right. It shifts because the culture changes.

And the engine of culture is status.

CHAPTER ELEVEN

Status, Dominance, and Affiliation

Baxter hates Truman

Baxter's my dog. He's a mutt, a gregarious, happy, expressive dog who manages to get along with just about every human and dog he meets.

Except for Truman.

Truman is the regal, self-assured German Shepherd who just moved in across the street. Truman's got a loving family, he goes for walks a few times a day, and he's driving Baxter crazy.

When Truman's fabulous family came over for dinner, they brought Truman along. Baxter freaked out. He couldn't control himself.

What's up with that?

Consider the penguins in the Galápagos. They spend about two hours a day fishing, and the rest of the time organizing themselves into a pecking order. There's an enormous amount of social grooming, of bumping, of social positioning.

And it's not just my dog and the penguins, of course.

It's us, as well.

It's not irrational; status makes it the right choice

Why do people choose one restaurant over another? One college? Why drive this car and not that one?

Why did that poker champion make a bad bet? Why rent a house instead of buying one? What club do you belong to?

If you look closely at decisions that don't initially make sense, you'll likely see status roles at work. The decision didn't make sense to you, but it made perfect sense to the person who made it.

We spend a lot of time paying attention to status.

Status roles: The Godfather and the undertaker

In his brilliant book *Impro*, Keith Johnstone helps us understand status roles, the hidden (but obvious) drivers of all elements of culture.

There's always an alpha dog in the pack. And every litter has a runt.

Status roles determine who gets to eat first in the lion pack, and who gets to drink first at the oasis.

In human culture, status roles are everywhere that more than one human is present. They exist in dating (who picks up the check) and in the boardroom (who comes in first, who sits where, who speaks, who decides, who's responsible).

My favorite example, one that captures the essence of Johnstone's point, is easily found if you visit YouTube and search for the opening scene of *The Godfather*.

In the scene, Amerigo Bonasera, the undertaker, a washed-out, tired, small man in a nondescript black suit, comes to visit the Godfather on the don's daughter's wedding day.

In just a few seconds, the stage is already set.

The low-status Bonasera (how could he be lower?) comes to visit the high-status Don Corleone, a man who has spent his entire life ensuring that he is on top of the status heap.

On this wedding day, though, the tradition is that the Godfather must grant any favor that is asked.

Over the course of just a few minutes of film, the universe is upended.

Bonasera asks Don Corleone to do violence to the men who have harmed his daughter. Family ties drive him to take a huge risk, to raise his status at the expense of the Godfather. To make things worse, he even offers to pay Corleone, transforming a patriarch into a hoodlum.

Oh, the tension.

In that moment, the undertaker's life is in jeopardy. He has gone too far. Parental pride has pushed him into a zone where the Godfather can't possibly operate. The Godfather can't grant this favor and maintain his status, and status is his lifeblood.

Through some remarkable directing jiu-jitsu, in just a few seconds, the normal order is restored, and the scene ends with the undertaker bowing to the Don and kissing his ring, pledging fealty.

Bonasera relieves the tension by returning to his place in the status hierarchy.

Status lets us

Status is our position in the hierarchy.

It's also our perception of that position.

Status protects us.

Status helps us get what we want.

Status gives us the leverage to make change happen.

Status is a place to hide.

Status can be a gift or a burden.

Status creates a narrative that changes our perceived options, alters our choices, and undermines (or supports) our future.

And the desire to change our status, or to protect it, drives almost everything we do.

Case Study: Lions and Maasai warriors

How do we save the lions of Kenya and Tanzania?

Conservation biologist Leela Hazzah saw how encroachments on their environment were making it more difficult for the lions to survive. But she also knew that among many Maasai, a rite of passage for adolescent males was to singlehandedly kill a lion. This show of bravery was putting significant pressure on the lion population. It's estimated that there are only thirty thousand lions in the region, down from two hundred thousand a generation or two ago.

All the rational arguments in the world aren't powerful enough to change deeply held cultural beliefs, even in this community. The need for status (as a parent, as a young adult) is within all of us. Instead, Dr. Hazzah and her team worked to create new cultural beliefs built on top of basic human desires.

As we learned from the quarter-inch drill bit, the action isn't always obviously connected with the desired emotion. In the case of the Maasai, the cultural goals are to bind the community to each other, to create feelings of empowerment and possibility, to inculcate bravery and patience, and to have a significant rite of passage. To raise the status of the boy as he becomes a man.

None of these goals are directly related to killing a lion. That was simply a historical artifact.

Working with and within the Maasai cultural systems, Dr. Hazzah and her team introduced a new rite of passage and built cultural influences around it. Instead of demonstrating bravery and patience by killing a lion, the young members of the culture now demonstrate those skills by saving one.

In their words, "Wildlife conservation has traditionally focused on wildlife, not people. At Lion Guardians, we take the opposite approach. For almost a decade, we have worked with local communities to protect lions and improve . . . community conservation by blending traditional knowledge and culture with science."

Now, the Maasai find and name lions, track them, and use radio telemetry to perform a census. Protecting a lion has become as much of a rite of passage as killing one used to be.

The status dynamic is always at work

Once seen, it can't be unseen. Say a cop pulls over a motorist for running a stop sign. Who has status in that situation?

That same motorist goes on to the office, where he barks orders at the receptionist. Who has status?

A clash of status roles happens in any bureaucracy that only knows how to measure today's status changes.

The roles we easily adopt at school—the class clown, the big man on campus, the A student—are status roles. And remember how hard we defended those roles, even when we had a chance to change them.

When the marketer shows up with her new idea, her opportunity, the offer to make change happen—every time, it's a challenge to our status. We have the choice to accept (and move up or down, depending on the story we tell ourselves) or to turn down the offer and live with the tension of walking away.

It's a mistake to believe that everyone wants to make their status higher. In fact, few people do. It's also a mistake to believe that no one wants to make their status lower. If you've been conditioned to see yourself in a certain status role, you might fight to maintain and even lower your status.

The smart marketer begins to realize that some people are open and hungry for a shift in status (up or down), while others will fight like crazy to maintain their roles.

Status is not the same as wealth

In some circles, a Pulitzer-winning columnist has far more status than I do. A doctor in charge of a prestigious hospital might have more status than a wealthy plastic surgeon. And the penniless yogi in a little village in India has more status than the richest man in town, at least to some of his peers.

In the last few decades, we've gotten lazier in our nuance of awarding status, preferring it to be related to either the dollars in a bank account or the number of followers online. But status continues to take many forms.

Six things about status

1. *Status is always relative.* Unlike eyesight or strength or your bank balance, it doesn't matter where you are on the absolute scale. Instead, it's about perception of status relative to others in the group. 6 is bigger than 4, but lower than 11. There is no highest number.

2. *Status is in the eyes of the beholder.* If you are seen as low status by outsiders but as high status in your own narrative, then both things are true, at different times, to different people.

3. *Status attended to is the status that matters.* Status is most relevant when we try to keep it or change it. For many people, status is upmost in our minds in every interaction. But it only matters when the person we're engaging with cares about status.

4. *Status has inertia.* We're more likely to work to maintain our status (high or low) than we are to try to change it.
5. *Status is learned.* Our beliefs about status start early. And yet the cohort we are with can influence our perception of our status in very little time.
6. *Shame is the status killer.* The reason that shame is used as a lever is simple: it works. If we accept the shame someone sends our way, it undermines our entire narrative about relative status.

We adjust our status constantly, intuitively playing with it based on the situation. And when you bring your work to the market, nothing is considered before status roles.

Frank Sinatra had more than a cold

Frank Sinatra lived two lives, deeply in conflict with one another. As chronicled by Gay Talese, the outside world saw him at an apex, the definition of suave and sophisticated. He was a high-status power broker, a serious man, the one and only.

When Frank looked in the mirror, though, he saw a low-status skinny kid, disrespected, barely holding on to what he had. He surrounded himself with yes men and sycophants, but still managed to have self-sabotaging tantrums and a miserable life that belied his fame, fortune, and good health.

When we bring status into our marketing, we are walking on very thin ice. We don't know if the person we're engaging with appears to have high status (and doesn't believe it) or actually believes and wants to increase his standing.

But it's not clear that we have much choice . . . because every big decision is made based on our perceptions of status.

Learning to see status

The idea of status isn't nearly as simple as it appears. Consider, for those you seek to serve, their external status (how they are seen by their chosen community) and their internal status (who they see when they look in the mirror).

Next, work through how they maintain or seek to change that status. Do they belittle others? Seek approval? Help in self-less ways? Drive themselves to achieve more? What sort of wins and losses do they track? Consider the following two XY grids.

People in the top-right quadrant (a) are rare indeed. This space belongs to people who are seen as powerful and who also see themselves as able to handle it. I'd put Oprah Winfrey in this category. This is the person who is able to choose, not the one who is waiting to be chosen.

The top-left quadrant (d) is more common, since people who end up with high status often doubt themselves. This can turn them into divas. The best stories about Frank Sinatra are about the juxtaposition of his perceived royalty status with his own need for affirmation. Impostor syndrome lies here.

The bottom-right quadrant (b) is for people who see them-

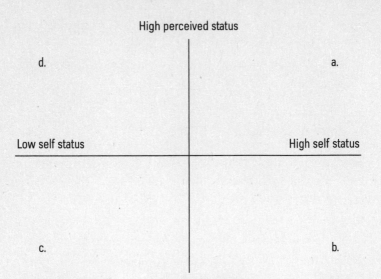

selves as far better than the rest of the world does. This is where you can find artistic drive and a willingness to strive for better. But over time, it can also lead to bitterness.

And finally, the bottom-left quadrant (c) is where we categorize people who see themselves as undeserving (and the world agrees). While this appears to be a sad place, it's also a consistent one, which is why we've embedded this role in the hierarchical culture. This is Cinderella before the ball, never expecting a chance for more. This is the coal miner, fighting to keep a dangerous, low-paying job.

Before we do the analysis, though, there's one more grid:

Seek to stay high/move up

4.   1.

Enable self/demean others   Enable others

3.   2.

Seek to stay low/move down

In many interactions, people seek to change their relative status—either to adjust themselves up in comparison to their peers, or to seek safety by giving up and moving down.

Moving down creates safety because there's more room and less threat. Fewer people jostle here for a better view or the chance to eat lunch first.

People are intensely aware of their relative status. We can move up or down. We can do that by helping/pushing others up or down. We can open the door for others and enable them to increase their status, or we can spend time denigrating others or increasing our own status.

In quadrant 1, we see the philanthropist, the committed teacher, and the social justice proponent. She seeks to improve her status with others by demonstrating the power to focus on those with low status instead of herself. This is certainly how Superman came to be understood by us. He could rob banks, but he saves lives instead.

In quadrant 2, we see similar behavior for a different reason. This is the person who not only lets other people ahead in line but doesn't even bother to try out for a role, because others are more deserving.

Quadrant 3 is the antisocial character who presents a noxious, infantile narcissism to the world. He's angry, he knows he can't measure up, but he's going to take down everyone around him. O. J. Simpson and Martin Shkreli are here.

And quadrant 4 is the hard-charging selfish person who desperately wants to win every engagement, and who is willing to do it with a combination of creating value and tearing down the competition.

Different stories for different people

We each have our own narratives. The noise in our head, the worldview that is unique to us, the history and beliefs and perceptions that shape who we are and what we choose. And sonder is the generous act of accepting that others don't want, believe, or know what we do—and have a similar noise in their heads.

But in order to bring our change to the world, we need to make some assumptions about what others believe. We can't hear the noise in their heads, but we can watch what they do and make some guesses.

There is a schism in our culture. In various moments, there are two sides that tell themselves very different stories and act them out in different ways: 1) the populations that default, in certain settings, to dominion, and 2) those that seek affiliation.

Affiliation and dominion are different ways to measure status

Every search on "nicest guy in Hollywood" brings up a picture of Tom Hanks. And every search on "The Godfather" brings us a picture of the fictional Don Corleone.

Tom Hanks cares about affiliation. Don Corleone measured domination instead.

Seeing the difference unlocks an understanding of our world, our political landscape, and how your customers might see things. This section of our journey is filled with personas, narratives, and exaggerations about each worldview.

Affiliation:
The questions that someone who cares about affiliation asks himself and those around him:

Who knows you?

Who trusts you?

Have you made things better?

What is your circle like?

Where do you stand within the tribe?

Can't we all get along?

Dominion:

The questions and statements that someone who cares about dominion offers to himself and those around him:

This is mine, not yours.

Who has more power?

I did this myself.

My family needs more of what we already have.

My side dominating your side means I don't have to be in charge, as long as my leader is winning.

On the ball field, a twelve-year-old might care about nothing but winning. And not just winning, but beating the opposition. He'll impugn the referee's motives, stomp on toes, and hold nothing back in order to win.

That same kid doesn't care at all about being at the top of his class, but he cares a lot about who sits next to him on the bus.

In the jazz band, someone is keeping track of how many solos he gets, and someone else wants to be sure she's helping keep the group in sync.

The people you're seeking to serve in this moment: What are they measuring?

If you want to market to someone who measures dominion or affiliation, you'll need to be aware of what's being measured and why.

"Who eats first" and "who sits closest to the emperor" are questions that persist to this day. Both are status questions. One involves dominion; the other involves affiliation.

Not simply eating first, but being on the same team as the person who eats first. And getting pleasure out of watching others eat last.

Not simply sitting near the emperor, but knowing that you'll be in his good graces (and those of the rest of the royal court) tomorrow as well.

Which is the narrative your audience resonates with?

Learning from pro wrestling

What is pro wrestling, really, but a battle for status?

It's not just among the wrestlers, but also among the fans. Because when your hero moves up, so do you.

If you can see the lens that pro wrestling and its fans use to see the world while they're at a match, you can understand how some people will view your offering as well.

The alternative to dominion is affiliation

One can gain status without an oil well or a factory. And one can enjoy as much status by letting someone into the flow of traffic as they can from cutting him off.

This is the status that comes from the community. It is the status of respect in return for contribution, for caring, for seeing and being in sync with others. Especially others with no ability to repay you.

Modern society, urban society, the society of the internet, the arts, and innovation are all built primarily on affiliation, not dominion.

This type of status is not "I'm better." It's "I'm connected. I'm family." And in an economy based on connection, not manufacturing, being a trusted member of the family is priceless.

Fashion is usually about affiliation

What are they showing? What is everyone else doing? Is this the season?

Within competitive markets, there is a race to be the dominant voice, but among the customers that make up that market, the position of leader works because the customers desire to be affiliated with one another.

The leader provides a valuable signal, a notice to expect that everyone else will be in sync. The goal isn't winning; it's being part of the group.

Sending dominance signals

Uber built its brand on dominance. The first few years of their rollout were marked by contentious relationships with local governments, competitors, and drivers. This signaling aligned with the view of some investors, employees, and users and per-mitted them to double down on their story and how it was told. There are some customers, partners, and employees who will respond best to a narrative of winning and losing.

What kind of company do you want to work for? People who align with one worldview often have trouble imagining why someone would choose the alternative.

Sending affiliation signals

Marketers spend an enormous amount of time and money on the simple task of sending affiliation signals. How busy is the trade show booth? Who else is at the launch party? Who blurbed the book? Are "people" talking about it (which is short-hand for "Are people like us doing something like this?")?

Affiliation isn't as focused on scarcity as dominion is, because affiliation admires the network effect. More affiliation leads to affiliation for everyone involved. Abundance is welcome.

The affiliated marketer seeking leverage works to prime the pump by sending the right signals to the right people, in search of a cascade. For an investment bank, that means running the tombstone ads with the names of all the "right" firms at the bottom. For a business-to-business seller, that means creating re-ferrals. For a local craftsperson, it means hunkering down in a single neighborhood until a reputation is assured.

Dominion is a vertical experience, above or below. Affilia-tion is a horizontal one: Who's standing next to me?

Affiliation or dominance is up to the customer, not you

Do you see the world in terms of winners and losers? Up and down? Or is it more about insiders and outsiders, being in sync, being part of a movement?

The way *you* see the world isn't nearly as important as the worldview of those you seek to serve.

As we've seen, their worldview is always stronger than the story you choose to tell. The people we seek to serve have a noise in their heads that's different than your noise.

CHAPTER TWELVE

A Better Business Plan

Where are you going? What's holding you back?

It's not clear to me why business plans are the way they are, but they're often misused to obfuscate, bore, and show an ability to comply with expectations. If I want the truth about a business and where it's going, I'd rather see a more useful document. I'd divide the modern business plan into five sections:

Truth	People
Assertions	Money
Alternatives	

The truth section describes the world as it is. Footnote if you want to, but tell me about the market you are entering, the needs that exist, the competitors in your space, technology standards, and how others have succeeded and failed in the past. The more specific, the better. The more ground knowledge, the better.

The more visceral the stories, the better. The point of this section is to be sure that you're clear about how you see the world, and that you and I agree on your assumptions. This section isn't partisan—it takes no positions; it just states how things are.

Truth can take as long as you need to tell it. It can include spreadsheets, market share analysis, and anything else I need to know about how the world works.

The assertions section is your chance to describe how you're going to change things. We will do X, and then Y will happen. We will build Z with this much money in this much time. We will present Q to the market, and the market will respond by taking this action.

You're creating tension by telling stories. You're serving a specific market. You're expecting something to happen because of your arrival. What?

This is the heart of the modern business plan. The only reason to launch a project is to make change, to make things better, and we want to know what you're going to do and what impact it's going to have.

Of course, this section will be inaccurate. You will make assertions that won't pan out. You'll miss budgets and deadlines and sales. So, the alternatives section tells me what you'll do if that happens. How much flexibility does your product or team have? If your assertions don't pan out, is it over?

The people section rightly highlights the key element: Who is on your team, and who is going to join your team. "Who" doesn't mean their resumes; it means their attitudes and abilities and track record in shipping.

You can go further here. Who are the people you're serving? Who are the champions? What do they believe about status? What worldview do they have?

The last section is all about money. How much you need, how you will spend it, what cash flow looks like, profit and loss, balance sheets, margins, and exit strategies.

Your local VC might not like this format, but I'm betting it will help your team think through the hard issues more clearly.

Perhaps you've seen the shift

When you opened this book, you probably said, "I have a product and I need more people to buy it. I have a marketing problem."

By now, I hope that you see the industrialist/selfish nature of this statement. The purpose of our culture isn't to enable capitalism, even capitalism that pays your bills, The purpose of capitalism is to build our culture.

Once you adopt a posture of service, of engaging with the culture to make change, the shift happens.

Now, instead of asking, "How can I get more people to listen to me, how can I get the word out, how can I find more followers, how can I convert more leads to sales, how can I find more clients, how can I pay my staff . . . ?" you can ask, "What change do I seek to make?"

Once you know what you stand for, the rest gets a lot easier.

A glib reverse engineering of your mission statement isn't helpful

Too often, we get hung up on our purpose, our why, our reason for being. And too often, that purpose is simply a backward way of saying, "I'd like to sell more of what I've already decided to sell."

In my experience, most marketers actually have the same "purpose." To be successful. To engage with people in a way that benefits both sides. To be respected, seen, and appreciated. To make enough of a profit to do it again.

That's your why. That's why you go to work.

Okay, got it.

But a better business plan takes that universal need and makes it specific—describing who and what it's for. It outlines the tension you seek to create, the status roles you're engaging with, and the story you're bringing that will make change happen.

That's not your purpose. It's not your mission. It's simply what you do.

If it doesn't work, that's okay. It doesn't mean you're without a purpose, or that your "why" is doomed. All it means is that you've ruled out one more route in your quest to matter.

Now you can find a new one.

CHAPTER THIRTEEN

Semiotics, Symbols, and Vernacular

Can you hear me now?

We communicate with symbols. The letters "C-A-R" aren't an icon of a car, or a picture of a car. They're a stand-in, a symbol that, if you know English, brings to mind a car.

Nike spent billions of dollars to teach millions of people that the swoosh is a symbol of human possibility and achievement, as well as status and performance.

And, if you're a designer, the typeface comic sans is a symbol of bad taste, low status, and laziness.

Marketers have the humility to understand that not everyone sees a symbol the same way, the awareness to use the right symbol for the right audience, and the guts to invent new symbols to be placed on top of old ones.

A hundred years ago, semiotics was in its infancy. It wasn't something done by a billion people a day, every day, as we market to each other online. Now, our ability to do this with intent (or with naïve intuition) can make the difference between success and failure.

What does this remind you of?

Busy people (you know, the kind of people you seek to change) don't care about your work as much as you do. They're not as up to date as you are, or as aware of the competitive landscape or the drama behind the scenes.

We scan instead of study.

And when we scan, we're asking, "What does this remind me of?"

This means that the logo you use, the stories you tell, and the appearance of your work all matter. Your words resonate with us, not only because of what they mean, but because of how they sound and how you use them.

It's not just the stuff. It's even the way you set up the room for your company off-site.

If it reminds us of a high school cafeteria, we know how to act. If it's a bunch of round tables set for a chicken dinner, we know how to act. And if there are row upon row of hotel-type chairs in straight lines, we know how to sit and act glazed.

We don't care about you, or how hard you worked on it. We want to know if it's for us, and if you're the real deal.

This is semiotics. Flags and symbols, shortcuts and shorthand.

Do the flashing lights at an arena rock concert change the way the music sounds? Perhaps they do, because they remind us we're at an arena rock concert.

When we hold a newspaper, it feels different than a tablet, or a comic book, or a Bible. The form changes the way the words sound.

A chocolate bar presents itself differently than a chemotherapy drug.

When we walk into a medical office that feels like a surgeon's office, we remember how that surgeon helped us . . . even if this office belongs to a chiropractor.

When we pick up a book that feels self-published, we treat it differently than the book that reminds us of a classic we read in high school.

When we get a phone call and hear the telltale clicks and pauses before the stranger begins to speak, we remember all the robocalls and phone spam we've gotten and hang up before the caller even utters a word.

And when the website is designed with GeoCities and flashing GIFs . . .

If you remind me of a scam, it will take a long time to undo that initial impression. That's precisely why so many logos of big companies look the same. It's not laziness. The designers are trying to remind you of a solid company.

That's the work of "reminds me of." You can do it with intent.

Hiring a professional

The internet is littered with websites, emails, and videos made by amateurs. Amateurs who made something that they liked.

Which is fine.

But what a professional does for you is design something that other people will like. They create a look and feel that reminds people of their sort of magic.

There's not one professional look, not one right answer. A summer blockbuster gives itself away in four frames of film—it's clearly not a YouTube video from a teen makeup guru.

Every once in a while, the amateur happens to find a vernacular that reminds the right people of the right story. The rest of the time, it's best to do it with intent.

Imagine that world . . .

Don LaFontaine made more than five thousand movie and TV voice-overs. It's not because he was more talented at speaking than anyone else, or because he was the cheapest. It's because his head start compounded, and if a studio chief wanted to remind the audience of a big-time movie, his voice could do that, precisely because he was reminding you of his earlier work.

It's important to remember that it doesn't matter what you, the marketer who created it, is reminded of. Semiotics doesn't care who made the symbol. The symbol is in the mind of the person looking at it.

And it's even more important to remember that there's no one right answer. The symbol that works for one group won't work for another. In Silicon Valley, the hoodie is a symbol of status (I'm too busy to go clothes shopping). In a different context, though, for a different audience, a hoodie in East London might put someone on alert instead of reassuring them.

Why is Nigerian spam so sloppy?

If you've gotten an email from a prince offering to split millions of dollars with you, you may have noticed all the misspellings and other telltale clues that it can't possibly be real.

Why would these sophisticated scammers make such an obvious mistake?

Because it's not for you. Because they're sending a signal to people who are skeptical, careful, and well-informed: go away.

The purpose of the email is to send a signal. A signal to the greedy and the gullible. Because putting anyone else into the process just wastes the scammer's time. They'd rather lose you at the beginning than invest in you and lose you at the end.

The flags on SUVs are called flares

In 2018, the more expensive a car is, the more likely it is to have slightly exaggerated flares around the wheels.

These flares are easier to make than they used to be (robots bending steel), but they remain a signifier. A message about the status of the car and its driver.

They have no real function. The flare is more than six inches away from the wheel. But they remain.

And in the aftermarket, you can pay extra for an even bigger flare, sort of surgical augmentation for your car.

Do that too much and your status goes down with most bystanders, not up. Just as it does with plastic surgery.

The Cadillac XTS goes even further. There is a tiny flare on the back of each tail light. Again, no useful purpose, except to remind some people, just a bit, of the Batmobile (or the 1955 Lincoln Futura).

These flags of status are everywhere we look.

Alex Peck points out that driving gloves have a big hole in the back. Why? Perhaps it's left over from when men with cars wore big watches, and the glove needed a hole to give the watch a place to poke through.

Over time, we forgot the big watch and just kept the hole. It's a symbol.

These leftover utilities have become symbols, and once a symbol becomes well known (like the tiny details on an Hermès handbag) it's quickly copied, manipulated, and spread, until it ceases to be scarce and then becomes merely a signal of changing taste.

What's your flag? Why would someone fly it?

The flag is not for everyone

It's worth restating that the smallest viable market gives you the freedom to pick those you seek to serve. And those people are seeking a certain symbol. It's likely, if you've chosen the market well, that the symbol they seek is quite different from one that would work for a larger audience.

There's a paradox here. If we want to make change, we need to go first, hanging over one edge or another. But often, that innovation reminds (some) people of a past event that went wrong. We begin by serving an audience that's okay with that, because it's the only audience that will give us a chance with our new thing.

Send a signal that feels like a sign we already trust, then change it enough to let us know that it's new, and that it's yours.

The same and the different

Most car ads look the same. That's because the sameness sends a signal about the car being worth considering, a safe alternative for such a huge investment.

Fashion ads in *Vogue* look nothing like the ads in *Field & Stream* or *Sports Illustrated*. Why? The vernacular matters. You're not people like us if you don't talk (talk means typefaces, photo styles, copy) the way we expect you to.

This is what a good designer offers you. The chance to fit in.

And sometimes, you might choose to hire a great designer instead. Someone who can break the expectation and talk differently, but not so differently that you don't resonate with those you seek to connect with.

When ad legend Lee Clow took the imagery from George Orwell's *1984* to create the most iconic TV commercial of all time, almost no one watching Apple's Super Bowl ad understood all of the references. (They'd read the book in high school, but if you want to impact a hundred million beer-drinking sports fans, an assigned high school book is not a good place to start.) But the media-savvy talking heads instantly understood, and they took the bait and talked about it. And the nerds did, and they eagerly lined up to go first.

The lesson: Apple's ad team only needed a million people to care. And so they sent a signal to them, and ignored everyone else.

It took thirty years for the idea to spread from the million to everyone, thirty years to build hundreds of billions of dollars of market cap. But it happened because of the brilliant use of semiotics, not technology. At every turn, Apple sent signals, and they sent them in just edgy enough words, fonts, and design that the right people heard the message.

Case Study: Where's Keith?

Not all semiotics are benign. When Penelope Gazin and Kate Dwyer started their site Witchsy.com, they had trouble getting their emails answered. They created a third partner, a fictional guy named Keith, gave him an email address, and had him initiate and participate in email threads.

This simple shift exposed a shameful gap in how our society treats women and men. Emails from "Keith" were quickly responded to. Vendors, developers, and potential partners were more likely to get back to Keith, addressed him by name, and were more helpful, they reported to *Fast Company*.

We're judging everything, and people are judging us in return. Often, those judgments are biased, incorrect, and inefficient. But denying them doesn't make them disappear.

The marketer can use symbols to gain trust and enrollment, or find that those symbols work in the opposite direction. To change the culture, we have no choice but to acknowledge the culture we seek to change.

That doesn't mean giving up, fitting in, or failing to challenge injustice. But it does require us to focus our stories and symbols with intent. Who's it for? What's it for?

We add the flags with intent

The semiotic flags we choose to fly are up to us. Not flying one is as intentional as flying one.

The people you are seeking to serve are trying to figure out who you are. If you're going to show up in their world, make it easy for them to know who you are and where you stand.

The lazy thing to do is insist that you don't need a flag (or a badge). That you don't have to nod your head to the cultural memes that came before, or even wear a uniform.

The foolish thing to do is pretend your features are so good that nothing else matters.

Something else always matters.

Are brands for cattle?

What's your brand?

Hint: it's not your logo.

In a super-crowded world, with too many choices (more than twenty kinds of toner to choose from for my laser printer, and more than nineteen thousand combinations of beverages at

Starbucks) and with just about everything "good enough," you're quite lucky if you have a brand at all.

A brand is a shorthand for the customer's expectations. What promise do they think you're making? What do they expect when they buy from you or meet with you or hire you?

That promise is your brand.

Nike doesn't have a hotel. If it did, you would probably have some good guesses as to what it would be like. That's Nike's brand.

If you have true fans, the only reason you do is because this group has engaged with you in a way that signals that they expect something worthwhile from you next time. That expectation isn't specific; it's emotional.

A commodity, on the other hand, has no brand. If I'm buying wheat by the ton or coffee by the pound or bandwidth by the GB, I don't have any expectations other than the spec. Get me exactly what I got yesterday, faster and cheaper, and I'll pay you for it.

How do we know that brands like Verizon and AT&T are essentially worthless? Because if we switched someone from one to the other, they wouldn't care.

If you want to build a marketing asset, you need to invest in connection and other nontransferable properties. *If people care, you've got a brand.*

Does your logo matter?

It matters less than your designer wants it to, but more than the typical committee realizes.

If a brand is our mental shorthand for the promise that you

make, then a logo is the Post-it reminder of that promise. Without a brand, a logo is meaningless.

Here's a simple exercise:

Make a list of five logos you admire. As a consumer of design, draw or cut and clip five well-done logos.

Got 'em?

Okay, here's my prediction: each one represents a brand you admire.

Almost no one picks a swastika or the clever glyph of the bank who ripped them off. That's because logos are so wrapped up in the brand promise that we imbue them with all the powers of the brand, ignoring the pixels involved.

Yes, it's possible for a terrible logo to adorn a fabulous brand (complicated mermaid, anyone?). Many of the best brands have no identifiable or memorable logo (Google, Sephora, and Costco come to mind). And of course, a quick glance at your Helvetica clip sheet shows that most brands couldn't be bothered:

No, you shouldn't phone it in or be careless. No, you shouldn't choose a logo that offends or distracts people. Yes, you should pick a logo that works in different sizes in different media.

But mostly . . . pick a logo, don't spend a ton of money or have a lot of meetings about it, and keep it for as long as you keep your first name.

CHAPTER FOURTEEN

Treat Different People Differently

In search of the neophiliacs

In any group of one hundred people, pick a measure (height, weight, IQ score, hair length, speed on the 50-yard dash, number of Facebook friends) and you'll discover a significant number clump around the average.

About sixty-eight of the hundred people will be close to the average. Another twenty-seven will be significantly further away, and four will be extreme outliers.

This happens often enough that we call it a standard deviation.

It turns out that this is especially true for human behavior.

Everett Rogers demonstrated that when it comes to style, technology, or innovations, most people like what they have. They want to do what others are doing, and they aren't actively seeking novelty.

Some people, though, the fifteen or sixteen people on the left side of the curve in the following graphic, are neophiliacs. They're early adopters. They want the better, the clever, the innovative. They'll wait in line to go to opening night of a movie, they'll upgrade their operating system right away, and they'll read *Vogue* magazine for the ads.

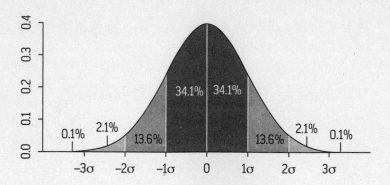

Standard deviations: The percentages indicate what percentage of the population being measured is in each segment. For example, 34.1% of the population is within one standard deviation below the mean.

And an equal number of folks, those on the right side of the curve, will defend their status quo to the last day. They still read *Reader's Digest* and use a VCR.

Good marketers have the humility to understand that you shouldn't waste a minute (not of your time or of their time) on anyone who isn't on the left part of the curve.

If someone is satisfied with what they have, you're unlikely to have the time or the money to reach out to them directly and cause them to become dissatisfied—that is, interested enough and open enough to changing and becoming a customer.

It's not for them. Not right now.

With persistence and smarts, you'll get to them, perhaps. One day. Horizontally. Person to person. Through earned media. But not right now.

It's the neophiliacs, the folks with a problem that you can

solve right now (novelty and tension and the endless search for better), that you can begin with.

Enrollment

There's no such thing as mandatory education. It's almost impossible to teach people against their will.

The alternative is voluntary education: gaining enrollment.

We ask people to eagerly lend us their attention. The promise is that it's worth their effort because, in exchange, they're going to get the insight or forward motion that they want.

Enrollment is what you need to earn permission to engage.

Enrollment is hands raised, eyes on the board, notes being taken. Enrollment is the first step on a journey where you learn from the customer and she learns from you.

Enrollment is mutual, it is consensual, and it often leads to change.

Lazy marketers try to buy enrollment with flashy ads. The best marketers earn enrollment by seeking people who want the change being offered. And they do it by connecting people to others who want the change as well.

And that change is precisely what marketers seek.

What do people want?

That's probably the wrong question.

Different people want different things.

Neophiliacs want to go first. They want hope and possibility and magic. They want the thrill of it working and the risk that it might not. They want the pleasure of showing their innovation to the rest of the crew. And they want the satisfaction of doing better work faster, as well as the anticipation of being rewarded for their innovation and productivity.

On the other hand, the typical corporate cog wants to avoid getting in trouble with the boss. And if trouble does happen, he wants an airtight alibi and a great way to avoid responsibility.

The social crusader wants a glimmer of hope and the chance to make things right.

The person who measures dominance instead of affiliation wants to win. And if he can't win, he might be willing to settle for watching his opponent lose.

The affiliation-seeking tribe member wants to fit in, to be in sync, to feel the pleasure of *people like us do things like this* without the risk of being picked to be the leader.

Some people want responsibility, while others seek to be recognized. Some of those you seek to serve want a bargain, while a few eagerly want to overpay, to prove that they can.

Almost no one wants to feel stupid.

More and more people have been seduced by the promise of convenience, so that they don't have to pay attention or exercise judgment. Others feel empty when they're unable to contribute effort.

The lesson: Always be wondering, always be testing, always be willing to treat different people differently. If you don't, they'll find someone who will.

The superuser

Some customers are worth more than others.

You've certainly heard the stories of restaurants that keep a picture of the local restaurant critic on the wall of the kitchen. The thinking is that if you can spot the critic early in the meal, you can raise the quality of the experience and get a better review.

If you can pull it off, this might be worth the effort.

The thing is, everyone is a restaurant critic now. Everyone can post on Yelp or share the experience with others. And so, the thinking goes, you need to treat everyone better because everyone has more power.

The math here doesn't hold up. Treating everyone better is a bit like treating everyone worse—given your resources, you can't treat everyone better than you already are. Instead, you can look at the new normal and realize that while everyone has a platform, not everyone is using it.

While everyone *could* be a neophiliac, a sneezer, a power user, a significant contributor, not everyone is taking that opportunity.

You can learn a lot about people by watching what they do. And when you find someone who is adopting your cause, adopt them back. When you find someone who is eager to talk about what you do, give him something to talk about. When you find someone who is itching to become a generous leader, give her the resources to lead.

We have the technological levers to treat different people

differently if we choose to. But we'll need to watch and listen to be able to figure out what to offer and who to offer it to.

The truth about customer contribution

It costs money to market.

It costs money to wear a suit to the meeting, to have a storefront, to develop new software, to keep your items in stock, to run ads, and to pay for publicity, and a hundred other things.

These are all fixed costs, all spread across your entire customer base.

If you do the math, what you'll see will look like this:

The dotted line is the amount you've spent per person on marketing. And the bars are how much gross margin you've earned from each customer.

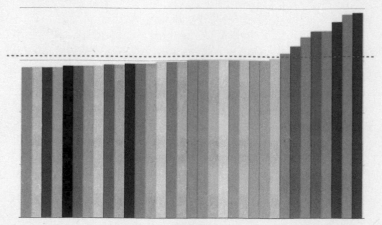

customers

Which means that only eight of the customers on this graph actually contributed a profit to your project.

The theory behind this graph is true for book buyers, restaurant goers, political donors, philanthropists, stamp collectors, and just about any industry where some customers spend more than others.

When you ask, "Who's it for?" the answer needs to be, "The kind of customers who are going to show up for us in a way that lets us keep going."

You'll serve many people. You'll profit from a few.

The whales pay for the minnows.

It can work out. But in order to do your best work, you'll need to seek out and delight the few. And in return, you'll be rewarded with a cadre of loyal customers who will buy in for all of it.

What's the purpose of this interaction?

Consider the valuable customer who reaches out to customer service about a problem.

How do we know if they're valuable? Well, the customer service folks have a record of who's writing or calling, so we begin there. A quick search shows that this person has been a customer for years, keeps a lot of money in your bank, tweets about you, never returns items, pays on time, buys your high-margin items, and so on.

In fact, if you do the math, you'll see that she produces eight times the revenue of the average customer, and unlike the anonymous masses that cost you money, she's one of the few who generate the income that actually turns a profit.

None of this would be an innovation if we were talking about a freelancer with six clients. When the big client calls, the freelancer instantly knows what's up.

But we're talking about your financial institution, the one where the least-respected and lowest-paid person is busy answering the phone when your customers call. Or your retail store, where the same thing is true.

In that moment, then, when the phone lights up, what's the interaction for?

If the goal is to get it over with, get the person off the phone, deny responsibility, read the script, use words like "as stated" and "our policy," then, please, sure, yes, keep doing what you're doing and watch it all fall apart.

On the other hand, the cost of being human in this situation is easily covered by the upside of delighting an extraordinary customer.

Get in your car, drive across town, and show up. Talk about it face to face.

Run down to FedEx and get that shipment in the last pickup of the day. Amazement and delight go a long way.

Have the CEO pick up the phone and call that customer that you accidentally triple-charged. It'll take a few minutes and it will be worth it.

I know you can't do it for every customer. But you can learn to see and act accordingly.

CHAPTER FIFTEEN

Reaching the Right People

Goals, strategy, and tactics

A brief aside before we get into more tactics.

Tactics are easy to understand because we can list them. You use a tactic or you don't.

Strategy is more amorphous. It's the umbrella over your tactics, the work the tactics seek to support.

And your goal is the thing you'll be betting will happen if your strategy works.

If you tell your competition your tactics, they'll steal them and it will cost you.

But if you tell them your strategy, it won't matter. Because they don't have the guts or the persistence to turn your strategy into their strategy.

Your goal is the change you seek to make in the world. It could be the self-focused goal of earning money, but it's more likely to be the change you seek to make in those you serve.

The goal is your shining light, the unwavering destination of your work.

Your strategy is the long-lasting way you're investing in reaching that goal. Your strategy sits above the tactics. A strategy might be to earn trust and attention. A strategy might be to be seen as the best and maybe only alternative. A strategy might be to have alliances and partnerships that enable you and your message to reach exactly the right people.

The way you use stories, status, and connection to create tension and forward motion is a strategy.

A strategy, if successful, gets you closer to your goal. You might need to change your strategy if it fails, but you don't want to do it often.

And the tactics? The tactics are the dozens or hundreds of steps you'll take on behalf of your strategy. If a tactic fails, that's okay, because another one can take its place and support the strategy you have in mind.

You can change tactics the moment you decide that they're not helping you achieve your strategy any longer.

For generations, Coca-Cola had a simple goal: get more people to drink more Coke. Their strategy was to run an enormous number of ads to persuade the mass market that Coke was part of the culture that made them happy—and that everyone else was drinking it too. And the ads kept changing, because the content of the ad was a tactic.

Patagonia's goal is to get a tiny group of outdoor enthusiasts to care about the environment and to express that care by wearing Patagonia apparel. In their words, "These are all silent sports. None require a motor; none deliver the cheers of a crowd. In each sport, reward comes in the form of hard-won grace and moments of connection between us and nature."

Their strategy is to redefine the way some people think about environmental impact as well as clothing quality. To give that small group a label and a tool they can use to evangelize their vision to their friends. To create insiders and outsiders.

And their tactics range from finding new ways to recycle clothes, to placing stores in brick buildings, to choices about materials, selection, and price. When a tactic fails, they don't abandon their strategy, the same one they've had for more than thirty years.

Advertising is a special case, an optional engine for growth

Media companies, telecommunication firms, and delivery services all make money doing the same thing: selling the attention of those they ostensibly serve.

You can buy an ad in a magazine, in an online network, or with a stamp. In all three cases, you'll be able to reach/interrupt/educate/engage with all the people the intermediary promised. Anyone with a stamp can send a letter.

You don't have to earn this attention, since you can buy it.

You're no longer the outsider; now you're the customer. You have cash and you can use it to buy attention, whenever you want, in as much quantity as you can afford.

Here's the good news: when you find an ad approach that works, you can scale it. You can scale it quickly and precisely.

And you've probably guessed the bad news: it's not easy to find an ad approach that works.

That doesn't mean you shouldn't try, but you need to be clear about what you're doing and why.

An ad, unnoticed, doesn't exist.

A noticed ad is noticed by some people, not everyone. And, if it's noticed by the right people, it creates tension. The tension of not knowing and needing to know more. The tension of being left behind. The tension that things might get better (or worse).

Almost all TV advertising is simply semiotic noise. Reassuring the viewer ("As seen on TV") that this is a safe brand, a brand you and your peers know, a brand that can afford to be on this box.

That's a tax that major companies in competitive markets have to pay. But it's not the sort of marketing that's realistic to consider for anyone else.

More than ever, but less than ever

More organizations run ads today than at any other time in history. If you've ever hit the "boost" button on Facebook, you're paying to be part of the ad business.

It's never been easier or cheaper to spend money to get the word out. You can pay LinkedIn for the privilege of sending an email to a bigshot, you can start by running free online ads for your nonprofit, and you can easily promote your conference or your bake sale.

There are three elements to the magic of online advertising:

1. You can reach people more precisely online than in any other medium. Not just the demographics of what they look like, but the psychographics of what they believe and what they're looking for.

2. You can reach people instantly. You can decide to run an ad at 10 a.m. and have it reach people beginning at 10:01 a.m.

3. You can measure everything.

Since advertising is faster, cheaper, and more measurable than ever before, why isn't this the focus of all our marketing? Why isn't this the beginning and end of the discussion?

Because online advertising is also the most ignored advertising ever created.

It's not unusual to run an ad in front of a hundred thousand people and get not a single click. It's not unusual for an entire ad campaign to start, run, and finish without making any impact on the culture.

Advertising is unearned media. It's bought and paid for. And the people you seek to reach know it. They're suspicious. They're inundated. They're exhausted.

You didn't pay the recipient to run that ad, but you want the recipient to pay you with their attention.

So you're ignored.

It's not that advertising can't work. It's simply that it's not the right answer for everyone, at least in this moment.

What does attention cost? What is it worth?

Please don't get distracted by the possibility of free attention, a spotlight that magically and generously makes you famous through no effort on your part.

Even "free" publicity costs you in terms of time and effort.

But for now, let's look at ads, where the equation of cost and attention is clear.

An ad in a fancy magazine will cost you $80 CPM, which means you get in front of 1,000 readers (using the term loosely) for eighty dollars. Or a bit under a dime per person.

An ad on a second-rate website might cost you $80 to be in front of a million people. But of course, these people are scanning, clicking, ignoring, and will neither remember your ad nor take action.

Anyone about to buy an ad needs to ask, "What's it worth?"

People seeking to make change happen are often in a hurry, and advertising feels like a shortcut. But without persistence and focus, the investment is wasted.

Brand marketing makes magic; direct marketing makes the phone ring

Lester Wunderman was the father of direct marketing. He named it and used it to build American Express, the Columbia Record Club, and a hundred other projects.

In 1995, I asked Lester to be on the board of Yoyodyne, the

online direct marketing company I founded before the world-wide web was a thing.

Lester was first in describing the differences between brand and direct marketing, but his ideas have never been more relevant. Thanks to the rise of Google and Facebook, there's now more direct marketing than ever before in history.

The difference is about what happens after the ad runs:

Direct marketing is action oriented. And it is measured.

Brand marketing is culturally oriented. And it can't be measured.

If you run an ad on Facebook and count your clicks, and then measure how many of them convert, you're doing direct marketing.

If you put a billboard by the side of the highway, hoping that people will remember your funeral parlor the next time someone dies, you're doing brand marketing.

It's entirely possible that your direct marketing will change the culture (that's a nice side effect). It may very well be that the ads you run, the catalogs you send out, and the visits to your site add up to a shift in the story that people tell themselves.

And it's entirely possible that your brand marketing will lead to some orders (that's another nice side effect). It may very well be that your billboard leads to someone getting off at the next exit and handing you money, or that your sponsorship of a podcast leads to someone hiring your company.

The danger is in being confused.

The extraordinary growth of Google's and Facebook's revenue

is due to only one thing: many of the ads that are run on these services pay for themselves. A hundred dollars' worth of online advertising generates $125 in profit for the advertiser. And she knows this, so she buys more. In fact, she keeps buying ads until they stop paying for themselves.

On the other hand, brand advertising (for products like Ford, Absolut Vodka, and Palmolive) shaped our culture for generations. But these brands and countless others can't possibly build direct marketing campaigns that work. And so the shift to a measured direct marketing environment online has been stressful and riddled with failure.

The approach here is as simple as it is difficult: If you're buying direct marketing ads, measure everything. Compute how much it costs you to earn attention, to get a click, to turn that attention into an order. Direct marketing is action marketing, and if you're not able to measure it, it doesn't count.

If you're buying brand marketing ads, be patient. Refuse to measure. Engage with the culture. Focus, by all means, but mostly, be consistent and patient. If you can't afford to be consistent and patient, don't pay for brand marketing ads.

The two paragraphs above ought to have paid for the time and money you've spent on this book. I'm hoping that's not the only thing that repays your investment, but even the biggest and most successful organizations are failing to see how the shift to online interaction is fundamentally changing their business.

Procter & Gamble spends billions on brand advertising on TV, for Tide and Crest and other brands. When TV brand ads are replaced with digital direct ads, their business model falls apart.

The local pizza place was hooked on Yellow Pages advertising. A big ad paid for itself, and the special phone number hooked up to the ad proved it. Moving to Yelp, on the other hand, is time consuming and feels risky. No control, no proven history.

For many smaller businesses, the move from expensive, slow, and difficult-to-measure brand ads to quick, agile, and measurable direct ads is a positive shift. But it's not easy to act like a direct marketer when you're trying to reach people who generally don't click on ads.

A simple guide to online direct marketing

The ad exists to get a click.

The click exists to either make a sale or earn permission.

The sale exists to lead to another sale, or to word of mouth.

Permission exists to lead to education and to a sale.

That's it.

Every step in the process has a cost (you paid cash at the first step, but along the way, you will lose some of those people who drop out), and every step also leads you closer to the benefit.

Assign values to each step. If you can't, don't run any direct-response ads until you can.

Will some people see your ads without taking action? Definitely. That's a side effect, a culture-shifting, awareness-building bonus. But if you can't measure it, it doesn't count.

A simple guide to brand marketing

Everything you do, from the way you answer the phone to the design of your packaging, from your location to the downstream effects of your work, from the hold music to the behavior of your executives, and even the kind of packing peanuts you use—all of it is a form of marketing your brand.

You can't measure it. You might not even notice it.

But it still matters.

You're already spending money on brand marketing. No doubt about it. The question is: What would happen if you spent a bit more? What if you spent it with intention?

If you could patiently invest more time and money in putting the story of your brand in the world, how would you do it?

You could certainly buy full-page ads in the local paper or put a commercial on network TV. There's a long tradition of this sort of spending. You can make a big statement in very little time. It's fun. It doesn't require buy-in from anyone except your boss or someone else with a budget. It's one and done, and you can move on to tomorrow.

It might be the best way to spend your money. Sponsoring a tennis tournament or a podcast might work wonders as well.

Maybe.

Or perhaps you should overinvest in the way your team interacts with customers. Or perhaps you should spend a few million dollars on research and development or go back to school to improve your craft.

The most important lesson I can share about brand marketing is this: you definitely, certainly, and surely don't have enough time and money to build a brand for everyone. You can't. Don't try.

Be specific.

Be very specific.

And then, with this knowledge, overdo your brand marketing. Every slice of every interaction ought to reflect the whole. Every time we see any of you, we ought to be able to make a smart guess about all of you.

Frequency

People don't remember what they read, what they hear, or even what they see. If they're lucky, people remember what they do, but they're not very good at that either.

We remember what we rehearse.

We remember the things that we see again and again. That we do over and over. We remember our Uncle Fred, who came to Christmas twenty years in a row, but we don't remember his date Ethyl, who came just that one time.

There are obvious evolutionary reasons we're optimized for this. We have to prune memories relentlessly, and the easiest memories to prune are the ones that are random noise.

We remember the events we have photos for in our family scrapbook, but don't remember the events that weren't photographed. It has nothing to do with the act of taking a picture and everything to do with rehearsing our story, the one we tell every time we see that picture.

Along the way, this has pushed us to associate "trust" with the events and stories that happen again and again. The familiar is normal and the normal is trusted.

Marketers forget this daily.

Because we get bored with our stuff. Our story, our change. We've heard it before. We remember it. But we're bored.

And so we change it.

Jay Levinson famously said, "Don't change your ads when you're tired of them. Don't change them when your employees are tired of them. Don't even change them when your friends are tired of them. Change them when your accountant is tired of them."

We can expand this well beyond ads.

All the storytelling you do requires frequency. You'll try something new, issue a statement, explore a new market . . . and when it doesn't work right away, the instinct is to walk away and try something else.

But frequency teaches us that there's a very real dip—a gap between when we get bored and when people get the message.

Lots of people start a project. They give a talk a few times, maybe even on the TED stage, and then they go off to do the next thing. They launch a new freelance business, get a few clients, then it sputters and they quit. Or they open a company, raise money and spend it fast, hitting the wall just before the good stuff happens.

The market has been trained to associate frequency with trust (there, I just said it again). If you quit right in the middle of building that frequency, it's no wonder you never got a chance to earn the trust.

Search engine optimization and the salt mines

The Google ecosystem is based on a myth. The myth is that millions and millions of businesses, all grooming themselves for the search engine, will be found by people who seek them.

Dating sites offer the same promise. As do the social networks.

Simply fit in all the way, follow all the rules, and when we search for "tire store" or "restaurant" or "freelance copy editor" or "fun weekend date," we will find you.

The math can't support this.

There are a thousand pages of results. What delusion we must be under to imagine *we* will be the first match.

The path isn't to be found when someone types in a generic term.

The path is to have someone care enough about you and what you create that they'll type in your name. That they'll be looking for you, not a generic alternative.

Yes, you can find my blog by searching for "blog" in Google. But I'd rather have you search for "Seth" instead.

SEO is the practice of ranking high in the search results for a generic term. A locksmith or a hotel or a doctor who wins their generic search will earn a huge profit. But everyone else is left to spend money on consultants and trickery to somehow rank higher. The math can't support this pyramid scheme.

On the other hand, a smart marketer can build a product or service that's worth searching for. Not the generic term, but to find you, the thing you built, the specific. When you do that, Google's on your side. They actually want *you* to be found when someone searches for you.

Step one is to make a product or service that people care enough to search for specifically. You cannot win in a generic search, but you'll always win if the search is specific enough.

And then step two is easy to understand: to be the one they want to find when they go looking.

CHAPTER SIXTEEN

Price Is a Story

Pricing is a marketing tool, not simply a way to get money

Eventually, you're going to have to tell people how much you're charging for your services and products. There are two key things to keep in mind about pricing:

Marketing changes your pricing.

Pricing changes your marketing.

Because people form assumptions and associations based on your pricing, and your pricing shapes what people believe about your service, it's important to be clear about how you position yourself. Your price should be aligned with the extremes you claimed as part of your positioning.

Are you the kind of person who buys the cheapest wine on the menu? What about the most expensive?

Notice that neither question said anything about the wine itself. Not about its taste or its value.

Simply the price.

No one drives the cheapest possible car (you hardly ever see a used Yugo going down the street) and few are foolish enough to drive a Bugatti around town. But within those extremes, count-less stories are being told. Stories we tell ourselves and stories we tell those around us.

A Porsche Cayenne has no conceivable utility proportionate to its expense. It's merely a signal, a silver or red painted flag we fly high in our driveway and in the theater of our self-esteem.

Of course, the price is more than a signal. It's also the engine for our project's growth, because price determines what we stand for, who we're designing for, and the story we tell. And price cre-ates (or eliminates) margin, and that margin is the money that's available to spend on our outbound marketing.

Consider the baker. If the ingredients and overhead associ-ated with a loaf of bread cost $1.95 a loaf at a reasonable quan-tity, we can examine three extremes:

At a retail price of two dollars a loaf, the profit per loaf is a nickel.

At a price of $2.50 a loaf, the profit per loaf is fifty-five cents. That's an eleven-fold increase, more than 1,000 percent more profit per loaf.

And at three dollars a loaf, we're making more than a dollar a loaf, more than twenty times what we made in the first example.

The baker who charges two dollars a loaf has to sell twenty-one loaves for every loaf the luxury baker sells at three dollars. Twenty-one times as many is the difference between a few cus-tomers an hour or a line out the door.

"But," we say, "our customers would prefer to pay the lower price."

Perhaps. But how do they value the sparkling clean shop, with plenty of well-paid and helpful staff, a new sign in the window, and a local baseball team with new jerseys with your logo on them? How do they value the handsome shopping bag that comes with every loaf, not to mention the free samples of the little butter cookies you call *punitions*? How does it make them feel to tell their friends that they're eating the same bread that's served at the fancy restaurant down the street?

Better to apologize for the price once than to have to excuse a hundred small slights again and again.

Price is a signal.

Different prices (different people)

The Quakers invented the price tag. Before that, it was generally accepted that nothing had a firm price. Everyone haggled.

But Macy's and Wanamaker's needed to get big, to build huge stores with low-paid staff. There was no way to train and trust that many people to haggle. And so they pioneered the Quaker idea at scale.

While the price tag was originally conceived because Quakers thought it was immoral to charge different prices to different people, it caught on because industrialists and big organizations liked the efficiency.

But, like everything else, the internet changes things.

On one hand, you can tell the story that the price is the price. Tesla told this story to luxury car buyers and they breathed a sigh of relief. But when Uber tried to match pricing to demand, it cost their brand billions in trust.

For most organizations, particularly small ones, the hard part isn't the mechanics of charging different amounts.

It's the storytelling.

I bring this up because it's a powerful way to understand the story of your price (and the price of your story). How do you feel when you find out that you got a discount that no one else got? What if you deserved it? How do you feel if other people got that discount and you didn't?

What about the scarcity and pricing built into Kickstarter? Does the fear of missing out on a level that's almost full push you to act?

"Cheap" is another way to say "scared"

Unless you've found an extraordinary new way to deliver your service or product, racing to be the cheapest probably means that you're not investing sufficiently in change.

When you're the cheapest, you're not promising change. You're promising the same, but cheaper.

The race to the bottom is tempting, because nothing is easier to sell than cheaper. It requires no new calculations or deep thinking on the part of your customer. It's not cultural or emotional. It's simply cheaper.

Low price is the last refuge of a marketer who has run out of generous ideas.

And what about free?

If marketing is done for and with the consumer, why not make everything free?

Two reasons:

1. Engaging in a transaction is fundamentally different than encountering an apparently worthless (or at least priceless) object that's been freely shared. Scarcity, tension, and enrollment all exist when we must decide to make a purchase, and the marketer sacrifices all of these when a purchase is truly free.
2. Without cash flow, you can't invest in your product, your team, or your marketing.

But free is worth considering for other reasons, in other situations.

Free is not simply a penny less than a penny, a dollar less than a dollar. It's an entirely different category of transaction, because like dividing by zero, it scales to infinity.

A free idea is far more likely to spread, and spread quickly, than an idea that's tethered to money.

If Facebook cost three dollars a month to use, it would have attracted fewer than a million users.

If it cost money to listen to the hits on the radio, the Top 40 would disappear.

And yet . . .

We don't know how to make a living if we give everything away.

The road out of this paradox is to combine two offerings, married to each other:

1. Free ideas that spread.
2. Expensive expressions of those ideas that are worth paying for.

When a chef gives away her recipes, or appears on a podcast, or leads an online seminar, she's giving her ideas away for free. It's easy to find them, engage with them with frequency, and share them.

But, if you want to eat that pasta served on china on a white tablecloth at her restaurant, it's going to cost you twenty-four dollars.

When a song on the radio is free, but the concert ticket costs eighty-four dollars, the artist can be compensated.

The china and the ticket are souvenirs of ideas, and souvenirs are supposed to be expensive.

There are countless ways for you to share your vision, your ideas, your digital expressions, your ability to connect—for free.

And each of them builds awareness, permission, and trust, which gives you a platform to sell the thing that's worth paying for.

Trust and risk, trust and expense

The rational thing is to believe that we're more likely to require trust before we engage in risky transactions.

And it's also rational to expect that people are more likely to want more trust before spending a lot of money (a form of risk). Or committing time and effort.

Many times, though, the opposite is true.

The fact that the transaction is risky causes cognitive dissonance to kick in. We invent a feeling of trust precisely because we're spending a lot. "I'm a smart person, and the smart thing to do would be to be sure I trust someone before investing my life savings (or my life), so I must trust this person."

That's what boot camp is for. The high cost of participation (blood, sweat, and tears) causes us to become aligned with the group.

That's why people change at Outward Bound.

That's why high-end restaurants and hotels can survive bad reviews.

When people are heavily invested (cash or reputation or effort), they often make up a story to justify their commitment. And that story carries trust.

Every con man knows this. The irony is that marketers who need to be trusted often don't understand it.

Lowering your price doesn't make you more trusted. It does the opposite.

Be generous with change and brave with your business

Generosity in terms of free work, constant discounts, and plenty of uncompensated overtime isn't really generous. Because you can't sustain it. Because soon you'll be breaking the promises you made.

On the other hand, showing generosity with your bravery, your empathy, and your respect is generous indeed.

What your customers want from you is for you to care enough to change them.

To create tension that leads to forward motion.

To exert emotional labor that will open them up to what's possible.

And if you need to charge a lot to pull that off, it's still a bargain.

Case Study: No tipping at USHG

For more than a decade, the best reviewed restaurant in the New York *Zagat's* guide was the Union Square Cafe.

Over the years, the company that operated the café added nearly a dozen other highly regarded restaurants around New York (and spun off Shake Shack, a billion-dollar company, in the process) as part of the Union Square Hospitality Group (USHG).

In 2016, they stunned a lot of observers by eliminating tipping.

Instead of accepting tips, USHG raised their prices 20 percent. They devoted the increased revenue to offering parental leave, fair wages, and the chance to treat their team as professionals. The shift meant that the folks in the back of the house (who actually cook your food) get paid better, and it means that the waitstaff have an incentive to work together, to trade shifts, to work the way a doctor, a pilot, or a teacher might—for the work, not for a tip.

This is great leadership, but it presents a host of marketing problems.

How do you communicate the price increase and elimination of tipping to a regular customer, someone who values the perception of a special relationship because he sees himself as an above-average tipper?

How to communicate this to a tourist, who is comparing menu prices online before making a reservation, and doesn't know that having tips included makes the restaurant much cheaper than it appears?

How to communicate this to the staff, particularly the highest-earning servers, who stand to see their wages go down?

What's the change being made, and who's it for?

One of the big insights to take away is that a change like this can't be for everyone. For example, some diners find joy in the status they get by leaving a big tip. They do it with a flourish, and, in the scheme of things for someone who's well off, it's a cheap thrill. USHG can't offer that thrill any longer. "It's not for you, sorry."

On the other hand, a diner seeking affiliation as a form of status can find that the right sort of sincere thank-you feels far better than the fear associated with tipping too little or too much.

Better still, the diner who has a worldview that revolves around fairness and dignity now has a harder time patronizing other restaurants. Given the choice between a restaurant where the workers are engaged, fairly treated, and working with dignity—or one where the hierarchy undermines all those things—it's easier to become a regular at a restaurant that is proudly aligned with your view of the world.

Dining in a restaurant is rarely a solo endeavor. USHG gives hosts a chance to gain status through virtue signaling. They give diners a story they can tell themselves (and others)—a story about how the small act of choosing a restaurant turns the ratchet on a much larger issue around race, gender, and income disparity.

That story isn't for everyone, but for the right people, it transforms the experience.

Who's it for, what's it for, and how is status changed? *What will I tell the others?*

CHAPTER SEVENTEEN

Permission and Remarkability in a Virtuous Cycle

Permission is anticipated, personal, and relevant

More than twenty years ago, in *Permission Marketing*, I narrated the beginning of a revolution.

It's about attention. Scarce attention.

Marketers had been stealing it, abusing it, and wasting it.

Spam was free, so spam some more. Spam, spam, spam.

Email spam, sure, but all sorts of spam. Constant efforts to steal our attention and precious time, which we can't get back.

There's an alternative. The privilege of delivering anticipated, personal, and relevant messages to people who want to get them.

That hardly seems controversial, but it was. It got me thrown out of the Direct Marketing Association.

What I saw twenty-five years ago was that spam didn't scale. That attention was truly precious, and selfish marketers needed to stop stealing something that humans couldn't make any more of.

My team and I built a company around this idea. At one point, Yoyodyne was sending, receiving, and processing more email than anyone else on the planet . . . and we were doing it with the active permission of every person we engaged with. Our open rates were over 70 percent and our emails averaged a 33 percent response rate.

That's about a thousand times the rate of a typical commercial email sent in 2018.

Before paying for ads, then, long before that, begin with the idea of earning this asset. The privilege of talking to people who would miss you if you were gone.

Permission marketing recognizes the new power of the best consumers to ignore marketing. It realizes that treating people with respect is the best way to earn their attention.

Pay attention is a key phrase here, because permission marketers understand that when someone chooses to pay attention they actually are paying you with something valuable. And there's no way they can get their attention back if they change their mind. Attention becomes an important asset, something to be valued, not wasted.

Real permission is different from presumed or legalistic permission. Just because you somehow get my email address doesn't mean you have permission to use it. Just because I don't complain doesn't mean you have permission. Just because it's in the fine print of your privacy policy doesn't mean it's permission either.

Real permission works like this: If you stop showing up, people are concerned. They ask where you went.

Permission is like dating. You don't start by asking for the sale at first impression. You earn the right, over time, bit by bit.

One of the key drivers of permission marketing, in addition to the scarcity of attention, is the extraordinarily low cost of connecting with people who want to hear from you. Drip by drip, message by message. Each contact is virtually free.

RSS and email and other techniques mean you don't have to worry about stamps or network ad buys every time you have something to say. Home delivery is the milkman's revenge: it's the essence of permission.

Facebook and other social platforms seem like a shortcut, because they make it apparently easy to reach new people. But the tradeoff is that you're a sharecropper. It's not your land. You don't have permission to contact people; they do. You don't own an asset; they do.

Every publisher, every media company, every author of ideas needs to own a permission asset, the privilege of contacting people without a middleman.

Permission doesn't have to be formal, but it must be obvious. My friend has permission to call me if he needs to borrow five dollars, but the person you meet at a trade show has no such ability to pitch you his entire resume, even though he paid to get in.

Subscriptions are an overt act of permission. That's why home delivery newspaper readers are so valuable, and why magazine subscribers are worth more than newsstand readers.

In order to get permission, you make a promise. You say, "I will do x, y, and z; I hope you will give me permission by listening." And then—this is the hard part—that's all you do. You don't assume you can do more. You don't sell the list or rent the list or demand more attention. You can promise a newsletter and talk to me for years, you can promise a daily RSS feed and talk to me every three minutes, you can promise a sales pitch every day (the way internet retailer Woot does). But the promise is the promise until both sides agree to change it. You don't assume that just because you're running for President or coming to the end of the quarter or launching a new product that you have the right to break the deal. You don't.

Permission doesn't have to be a one-way broadcast medium. The internet means you can treat different people differently, and it demands that you figure out how to let your permission base choose what they hear and in what format.

If it sounds like you need humility and patience to do permission marketing, that's because it does. That's why so few companies do it properly. The best shortcut, in this case, is no shortcut at all.

How many people would reach out and wonder (or complain) if you didn't send out that next email blast? That's a metric worth measuring and increasing.

Once you earn permission, you can educate. You have enrollment. You can take your time and tell a story. Day by day, drip by drip, you can engage with people. Don't just talk at them; communicate the information that they want.

Shortly after *Permission Marketing* was published, Dany Levy started an email newsletter called DailyCandy. It was a city-focused email alert for young women looking for local sales, parties, and connections. The asset was so valuable that she ended up selling it for more than a hundred million dollars.

And every podcaster has an asset like this, a subscriber base that regularly listens to the latest show.

And every successful politician has an asset like this, a group of activist voters eager to hear the next riff and share it or take action.

Protect it. It's more valuable than the laptops or chairs in your office. If someone walked out the door with those, you'd fire them. Act the same way if someone on your team spams the list just to make a metric go up.

Earn your own permission and own it

When we use a social media platform because it has plenty of users built in, we're not really building an asset.

Sure, for now you can reach your followers on this platform. But over time, the platform makes money by charging you, not by giving away their work.

And so you'll need to boost a post. Or worry about what happens when the platform tries to increase its stock price.

If permission is at the heart of your work, earn it and keep it. Communicate only with those who choose to hear from you. The simplest definition of permission is the people who would miss you if you didn't reach out.

You should own that, not rent it.

Tuma Basa and RapCaviar

In 2015, in a defensive move, Spotify hired music tastemaker Tuma Basa to compete with Apple's new initiative in DJ-curated playlists. Basa took over the RapCaviar playlist and within months, it had grown to more than three million subscribers. Those are listeners who have given permission to Spotify (and Basa) to share new music with them.

Within three years, he had grown the list to nine million people.

He built the most important asset in the music business. Bigger than any radio station. More important than any magazine.

When Basa profiles a new artist, she becomes a superstar (that's a money move, Cardi B). Every Friday morning, the playlist is updated, and by the end of the day, the landscape of hit music has changed.

Spotify doesn't need to own radio spectrum, or a magazine. They own a permission asset instead. Permission, attention, and enrollment drive commerce.

Showing up with generosity

How do you get permission in the first place? How do you connect with people who want to hear more from you?

The worldview of those who care about new things (the neophiliacs) drives them to seek out new voices, new ideas, and new options. There aren't a lot of these folks in your market, but there may be enough of them.

When Marvel wants to launch a new superhero franchise, they don't begin with nationwide TV ads. Instead, they go to San Diego Comic-Con.

The Comic-Con has permission. Permission from raving fans, neophiliac fans, to break new ideas, to help them find the next big thing.

That's the place to launch *Deadpool*. Not with a pitch, but with generosity.

A special coming attraction.

An interview with the director.

Actual news.

The movie's not coming out for a year. They're not there to sell tickets. They're there to earn permission. To gain attention over time, to earn the privilege of telling their story to people who want to hear it.

Mostly, it's a signal. A way of telling the core of the tribe that attention has been paid, that this is the sort of thing people like us will be talking about next year.

It doesn't matter that there's only a tiny percentage of the movie market at Comic-Con. What matters is the quality of their story and the depth of their empathy and generosity.

And then, if they've done it right, the word will spread.

Transform your project by being remarkable

It's almost impossible to spread your word directly. Too expensive, too slow. To find individuals, interrupt them, and enroll them, one by one . . . it's a daunting task.

The alternative is to intentionally create a product or service that people decide is worth talking about.

I call this a Purple Cow.

It's worth noting that whether something is remarkable isn't up to you, the creator. You can do your best, but the final decision is up to your user, not you.

If they remark on it, then it's remarkable.

If they remark on it, the word spreads.

If the conversations move your mission forward, then others will engage with your idea and the process continues.

Easier said than done.

You must do it with intent, building it deep into the product or service.

That means that effective marketers are also in charge of the experience that the customers have.

Offensive/juvenile/urgent/selfish is not the same thing as purple

Too often, impatient marketers resort to stunts. Stunts come from a place of selfishness.

You do people a service when you make better things and make it easy to talk about them. The best reason someone talks about you is because they're actually talking about themselves: "Look at how good my taste is." Or perhaps, "Look at how good I am at spotting important ideas."

On the other hand, if we're going to criticize you, censure you, talk about how you've crossed a line, we're doing that to send a signal to our friends and neighbors. That you're to be shunned, that you're making things worse. We're not impressed by how much money you spent, what lines you crossed, or how important the work is to you.

No, we spread the word when it benefits us, our taste, our standing, our desire for novelty and change.

Suspending *Fight Club* rules

Chuck Palahniuk wrote that the first rule of Fight Club is that you don't talk about Fight Club.

As soon as the right sort of character (worldview!) in the novel heard about Fight Club, that rule was an invitation to talk about Fight Club. And, as it grew, so did the conversations. Metcalfe's Law again.

Alcoholics Anonymous is a huge organization. And it's hardly anonymous. Built into the practice of an active member is the posture that, when in doubt, we talk about AA, because talking about it is a generous act. It's a shame killer. It's a life raft. It's a fellowship of connection, a chance to do for others what was done for you.

Ideas travel horizontally now: from person to person, not from organization to customer. We begin with the smallest possible core and give them something to talk about and reason to do so.

What we choose to market is up to us. If the change you seek to make can't be talked about, perhaps you should find a different change worth making.

Designing for evangelism

Some members of AA bring tension to nonmembers. They eagerly (and generously) approach people with a drinking problem and offer to help.

Social pressure made us ill, they may think, and social pressure can make us better.

Evangelism is difficult. Bringing tension to a coworker or friend is fraught with risk. It's easier to avoid.

The hard work of creating the change you seek begins with designing evangelism into the very fabric of what you're creating. People aren't going to spread the word because it's important to you. They'll only do it because it's important to them. Because it furthers their goals, because it permits them to tell a story to themselves that they're proud of.

CHAPTER EIGHTEEN

Trust Is as Scarce as Attention

What's fake?

The internet thrives on affiliation. At its core is the magic that comes from peer-to-peer connections.

But the forces that prefer dominion instead of affiliation see this as a threat. And they've created waves of distrust around the voices and channels that we built our cultural trust around.

In addition, alas, the exposed misbehavior and greed of many of the pillars we count on have also destroyed the benefit of the doubt we'd like to give those who we look to for leadership.

The result is a moment in time when *more people are connected and fewer are trusted.* When science and fact are often thrown into a blender of willful misinterpretation and hurried misunderstanding. We're not supposed to trust spiritual institutions, the mainstream media, politicians, social networks, or even the person down the street.

Add to this the cacophony of noise (with less signal than ever before) and the prevalence of fakes and rip-offs, and trust is endangered.

What's trusted, who's trusted?

Into this vacuum of mistrust, marketers find themselves on one of three paths:

Ignored

Sneaking around

Trusted

If you're ignored, you can't accomplish much, because in addition to not earning trust, you haven't earned attention either.

If you're sneaking around, pretending to be one thing while acting in a different way, you might be able to steal some attention and earn some faux trust, but it won't last.

The third method—trust—is the only one that pays for the investment required. And it's nice that it's also the easiest to live with.

A trusted marketer earns enrollment. She can make a promise and keep it, earning more trust. She can tell a story, uninterrupted, because with the trust comes attention. That story earns more enrollment, which leads to more promises and then more trust. And perhaps, if the story is well organized and resonates, that leads to word of mouth, to the peer-to-peer conversations that are at the heart of our culture.

Benefit of the doubt is not a myth. There's a ton of doubt, and you're likely not getting the benefit of it. It's only when people are actually going where they think you're going, when their identity and status are already on the line—that's when you get the benefit.

And then change happens.

The trust of action

In a world that scans instead of reads, that gossips instead of re-searching, it turns out that the best way to earn trust is through action.

We remember what you did long after we forget what you said.

When we asked for a refund for a defective product, what did you do? When you lost our data, what did you do? When you had to close the plant and our jobs were on the line, what did you do?

Marketers spend a lot of time talking, and on working on what we're going to say. We need to spend far more time *doing*.

Talking means focusing on holding a press conference for the masses.

Not talking means focusing on what you do when no one is watching, one person at a time, day by day.

Famous to the tribe

Fame breeds trust, at least in our culture.

Everyone is famous to fifteen hundred people.

Some people are even famous to three thousand.

And that's a fascinating new phenomenon. When there are

three thousand or ten thousand or five hundred thousand people who think you're famous . . . it changes things. Not simply because they've heard of you, but because people they trust have heard of you as well.

If you're a business consultant, a designer, or an inventor, being famous to the right three thousand people is plenty.

The goal isn't to maximize your social media numbers. The goal is to be known to the smallest viable audience.

Public relations and publicity

Usually, marketers seek publicity. They want clips. Write-ups. Features. Getting the word out. If you hire a public relations firm, it's more likely that you're hiring a publicist.

And good publicity is great if you can get it—why not?

But what you probably need more than publicity is public relations.

Public relations is the art of telling your story to the right people in the right way. It willingly turns its back on publicity that seeks ink at all costs ("As long as they spell my name right") in exchange for the marketer's reliance on building an engine for an idea.

The race to be slightly famous is on, and it's being fueled by the social and tribal connections permitted by the internet. We give a lot of faith and credit to the famous, but now there are a lot more of them. Over time, once everyone is famous, that will fade, but right now, the trust and benefit of the doubt we accord the famous is quite valuable.

CHAPTER NINETEEN

The Funnel

Trust isn't static

Visualize a funnel, one with a bunch of leaks and holes in it.

At the top of the funnel, you pour attention.

At the bottom of the funnel, committed loyal customers come out.

Between the top and the bottom, most people leak out. They walk away, trust diminished, or leave due to a mismatch between what you offer and what they believe, a disconnect between what you say and what they hear. Or maybe it's just not a good fit, or they're distracted, or life got in the way.

As people work their way through the funnel—from stranger to friend, friend to customer, customer to loyal customer—the status of their trust changes.

Perhaps they become more trusting, the result of cognitive dissonance and experience. Or, more likely, they become more distracted, more fearful, more eager to run away, because saying yes is more stressful than simply walking away.

You can fix your funnel

1. You can make sure that the right people are attracted to it.
2. You can make sure that the promise that brought them in aligns with where you hope they will go.
3. You can remove steps so that fewer decisions are required.
4. You can support those you're engaging with, reinforcing their dreams and ameliorating their fears as you go.
5. You can use tension to create forward motion.
6. You can, most of all, hand those who have successfully engaged in the funnel a megaphone, a tool they can use to tell the others. *People like us do things like this.*

Funnel math: Casey Neistat

Casey regularly gets more than ten million views for one of his YouTube videos. That's a permission asset. People follow him and those people are likely to share his work.

For a recent project, he sent his viewers (when I saw the video, it had received about a million views) to his live stream on Twitch.

I clicked on the link and saw that it had been seen eighteen thousand times. So, about one in fifty people had clicked over.

On the Twitch video, there were hundreds and hundreds of comments. It's difficult to count, but let's call it a thousand.

Which means that one out of eighteen people took the time to post a comment.

And of the thousand commenters, perhaps five will go ahead and take further action like sign up for whatever Casey's building.

1,000,000 to 18,000 to 1,000 to 5.

That's what a funnel looks like. Your mileage may vary.

The reason that he's Casey and we're not isn't because he has optimized his funnel. It's because the top of the funnel is regularly and effortlessly filled with people who are enrolled in his journey.

Everything gets better once you earn that trust.

The sustainable direct marketing funnel

There's a special case here, a funnel that is now sought after by the millions who buy ads from Google and Facebook.

In 2017 these two companies took in more than a hundred billion dollars, about *half* of all the money spent on online advertising worldwide. And just about all of those ads were measured, and all of them involved the funnel.

Spend a thousand dollars on online ads that reach a million people.

Get twenty clicks.

That means that each click cost fifty dollars.

Those clicks go to your website. One out of ten turns into an order.

Which means that each order cost you five hundred dollars.

If you're fortunate, in this business we're describing, the lifetime value of a customer is *more* than five hundred dollars, which means you can turn around and buy more ads to get more customers at the same cost. And do it again, and again, with all the ads paying for themselves. Magic!

Of course, the vast majority of your profit is going straight from you to the place you're buying the ads, which is why those two companies are so extraordinarily successful. They're skimming the profit off the top of just about all of their advertisers. Google might make a hundred dollars per sale in profit, where you, the advertiser doing all the work, are making just ten dollars.

But you can live with that, because the margin on that next sale is still positive. Since you come out ahead, it's easy to buy more ads.

And the funnel ratchets forward.

This is the direct marketer's dream. It's advertising that clearly pays for itself. It lets you scale. You can measure what's working, do it again and again, and grow.

It's worth noting that very few organizations do this math carefully. They're spending and praying, hoping it all comes out in the wash.

But if you're careful and alert, you can begin to understand what putting attention into the top of the funnel costs you, and you can work to improve not only the quality of your leads but the efficiency of the process.

By all means, work to lower the cost of that first click. But if you do it by making a ridiculous promise in the ad you run, it'll backfire, because once in the funnel, people will stop trusting you, the tension will evaporate, and your yield will plummet.

Instead, consider focusing on which steps to shift or eliminate. Explore what happens if people engage in your ideas or your community *before* you ask them to send you money. Invest in the lifetime value of a customer, building new things for your customers instead of racing around trying to find new customers for your things.

When I started out in marketing, I'd guess that fewer than 5 percent of all advertisers measured their results. It was just too difficult to do with TV, radio, and print. Today, I'm guessing the number is closer to 60 percent, because the numbers are so clearly marked. What's missing is a thoughtful analysis of what those numbers mean.

An aside on funnel math

I'm not sure why funnel math flummoxes so many people, but if you take it step by step, you'll see it.

The most important thing to figure out is the lifetime value of a customer. Here's a simple example: What's a new loyal customer worth to a supermarket?

If all we do is calculate the profit on a single trip to the store, it's only a dollar or two. Supermarkets have very low margins.

But what if that person becomes a regular shopper? What if he visits twice a week, buying a hundred dollars' worth of groceries each time, and does so for the five years he lives in the neighborhood (not unusual in many suburbs)? That's fifty thousand dollars or more in sales. Even at a 2 percent profit margin, it means that there's a thousand dollars in profit from each new customer over time.

And . . .

What if your supermarket is special, and once someone becomes a shopper, there's a chance that they'll tell friends and neighbors and one of them will also become a regular shopper? That makes each new customer even more valuable, because they become your engine of growth.

This means that a supermarket should be eager to sponsor an event for new residents in town, because the funnel is so efficient.

And it means a supermarket ought to quickly give an apology and refund to a customer who's upset about a four-dollar melon not being ripe. It's hardly worth a thousand dollars in lost sales to have an argument.

With technology and services, we can go further. If we look at a service like Slack, an early customer might have had a lifetime value of fifty thousand dollars or more. If we count not only what they'd be paying over time, but also the impact on what their coworkers might end up paying, plus the value of growth in shutting out competitors, plus the value of the equity in the company once it was seen as the winner, it's easy to justify that sort of analysis. The first thousand customers, if they're the right people, are practically priceless.

Okay, so if that's the lifetime value, what does the funnel look like, the cost part of the equation?

The simplest way to think about this is with stamps.

If a stamped letter costs fifty cents out the door, how many letters do you need to send to get one customer?

In the old days of direct mail, that's all we needed to know.

If you need to send a thousand stamped letters to get one order, that means each order costs you five hundred dollars. (Because they cost fifty cents each, right?)

If your lifetime value of a customer is seven hundred dollars, *buy as many stamps as you can possibly afford!* On the other hand, if the lifetime value of a customer is four hundred dollars, you have no business buying stamps. You need a better letter or a better business.

That simple analysis is why you've heard of L.L. Bean, Lands' End, and Victoria's Secret. They bought a lot of stamps.

The internet makes this faster, more powerful, and more nuanced.

On the internet, you don't buy stamps from the post office. Instead, you buy clicks from Google or Facebook.

Those clicks go to a website.

That website click goes to another part of the website.

Or to an email.

Or to a trial download.

And then that leads to the next thing, and on and on until you've turned that interest into a paying customer.

Every click between the first and the last makes your funnel more expensive, but if you get rid of too many clicks then no one will trust you enough to buy from you.

If your product or service makes things better, the customer will stick with you and you'll generate that lifetime value we spoke of.

If you can't see the funnel, don't buy the ads.

If you can measure the funnel and it costs too much for you to afford ads, don't buy the ads. Fix the funnel first.

The truth about your funnel

It's not going to be a magical fountain of results.

I hope it will, but it's pretty unlikely.

While there are plenty of people happy to sell you a miracle— a self-running, passive funnel of income—these magical funnels are rare.

That's because the lifetime value of a new customer rarely exceeds the cost of running the ads necessary to get a new customer.

People are so distrustful, and the web is so cluttered, that the ads rarely have enough power to pay for themselves. People see so many ads, with so many promises, that the cost of engagement has gone through the roof.

The truth is that most brands that matter, and most organizations that thrive, are primed by advertising but built by good marketing. They grow because users evangelize to their friends. They grow because they are living entities, offering ever more value to the communities they serve. They grow because they find tribes that coalesce around the cultural change they're able to produce.

The work you put into improving your funnel is effort well spent. But attempts to build a perpetual motion machine of profit almost always end with bitterness, because they require you to push too hard and too fast to do anything that lasts.

The goal is to prime the pump with ads that are aimed at neophiliacs, people looking to find you. Then build trust with frequency. To gain trial. To generate word of mouth. And to make it pay by building a cohort of people, a network that needs your work to be part of who they are and what they do.

It's easy to skip the last part, the stuff that happens after the first click. And if you only do the easy, expensive part, you'll almost certainly be unhappy with the outcome.

Life on the long tail

Chris Anderson's breakthrough work on the long tail can be easily understood with a simple graph:

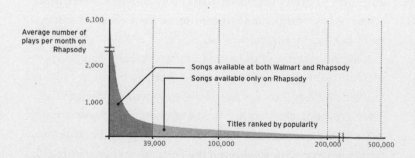

[credit: Chris Anderson]

On the left are the hits. There aren't many of them, but they each sell a lot. In fact, number one sells ten times as many copies as number ten, and a hundred times as many as number one hundred. A hit is magical.

On the right are the rest. The long tail: good products of specialized interest. Each, by itself, doesn't sell many copies, but taken together, the long tail sells as much as the short head.

Half of Amazon's sales are books that are not in the top five thousand. Half!

Half of the music consumed on streaming sites isn't available in stores. Not half the titles, half the volume.

Amazon can do great with this strategy since they sell *all* the available books. Each author, though, is in pain: selling one or two books a day is no way to make a living.

If you're a musician, living on the long tail with your twelve or twenty-four songs is not going to pay any bills. And almost everyone who publishes to an open marketplace is on the long tail.

Below, you'll see a similar graph showing traffic to websites. If you're at the circle, or worse, to the right of that circle, you can't compete for impact or ad dollars, because even though Google profits from every website they search, most of the people out on the edges are huffing and puffing.

These huge marketplaces (Amazon, Netflix, iTunes, etc.) depend on the misguided hopes and dreams of individuals way out on the long tail. Separately, each one struggles. Taken together, it's a good business.

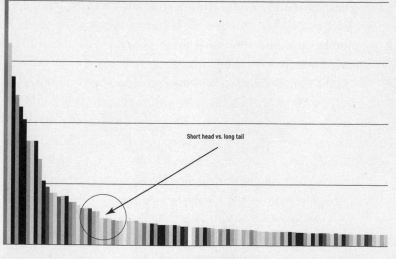

Traffic to the most popular websites

The April Fools' Passover Birthday Easter shirt

Here's a vivid example of living on the long tail: The other day I saw a T-shirt for sale on Amazon that said "It's Easter, It's Passover, It's April Fools', and It's My Birthday."

That's obviously a special-interest item, one that can't possibly support the effort that went into it. After all, only one in 365 people qualifies to wear a shirt like that, and perhaps one in a thousand of those would actually wear one, and, I don't know, perhaps one in a hundred of their friends would think to search for it, so the vendor probably sold four.

But there it was.

More searching found shirts like this one:

Oh, I see. It's a long-tail business. A few companies are making tens of thousands of different shirts. They're making them to order. The long tail and the infinite shelf space of Amazon makes this possible. They might not sell many (any) of any *particular* shirt, but taken together, it's reasonable to assume that they're selling thousands of shirts a month.

If you can aggregate a chunk of the long tail, you can make a go of it. But you can't possibly sell just one obscure shirt and have a shot.

This is the false promise of the internet. That you can be happy with a tiny slice of the long tail. That anyone can sing or write or dance or do comedy or coach or freelance, and so anyone will, and so you'll be fine.

Except you won't be fine, because you can't live on that. The internet can live on that, Upwork and Fiverr and Netflix and Amazon can live on that, but you can't.

We hear about the outliers, the kids who make millions of dollars a year with their YouTube channel or the fashionista with millions of followers. But becoming an outlier isn't a strategy. It's a wish.

There's a way out

The math of a hit is about more than the benefit of selling a lot of copies. Actually, hits are hits because people like hits.

We like to do what everyone else is doing.

(*Everyone* means "everyone like us.")

You've probably guessed the strategy: by dividing the market into many curves, not just one, we end up with many short heads and many long tails.

There's the market for literary fiction aimed at teenagers. The market for books on chip carving. The market for video courses on using a GH5 camera to make movies. And the market for performing improv.

There's even the market for drone music played so loudly that the audience needs to wear ear protection.

In each of these markets, and a million others, there's a need for a short head, at least once someone has connected the people in that market to one another, so they realize that they exist, so they see each other, and so they understand what the hit is.

Because it's the hit that connects them.

Once they see it, they'll probably want it.

This means that living on the long tail has two essential elements:

1. Creates the definitive, the most essential, the extraordinary contribution to the field.
2. Connects the market you've designed it for, and helps them see that you belong in the short head. That this hit is the glue that holds them together.

Rocky Horror is in the short head. So is the DeWalt 20V Max XR lithium ion brushless hammer drill.

It's the hit that unites us. The one that makes it clear that you are people like us.

Yes, the internet is a discovery tool. But no, you're not going to get discovered that way.

Instead, you will make your impact by uniting those you seek to serve.

Bridging the chasm

We have no idea who discovered the pothole, or who named the Grand Canyon, but Geoff Moore discovered the chasm. It's the overlooked but often fatal gap in the Rogers curve, the curve of how ideas spread through the culture.

The early adopters go first; they buy things because they're new, interesting, and a little bit risky.

They do that because they *like* things that are new, interesting, and little bit risky.

But there's a problem. There aren't enough of these neophiliacs to go around. Big organizations, mass movements, and substantial profits often depend on the mass market—they need action from the rest of us.

The mass market is where Heinz and Starbucks and JetBlue and The American Heart Association and Amazon and a hundred others live.

How do you get there?

The intuitive answer is that the early adopters will bring your idea to the masses and you'll be done.

But often, that's not what happens.

It doesn't happen because the mass market wants something different from what the early adopters want. The mass market wants *something that works*. Something safe. A pattern match, not a pattern interrupt. They take "people like us do things like this" very seriously.

Moore's point was that few innovations glide from one part of the market to the other. That's because in order to satisfy the early adopters, you may just need to annoy the masses. The very thing your innovation did (break things) is the one thing that the mass market doesn't want to happen.

They don't want to trade in their DVDs. They don't want to learn a new software platform. They don't want to read their news online.

To understand how this collision feels, go spend an hour or two at the help desk at the Apple store. Check out who's there and why. Listen to their questions, and pay attention to their facial expressions.

The middle of the curve isn't eagerly adopting. They're barely adapting. That's why they've chosen to be in the middle of the curve.

Where's your bridge?

The bridge across the chasm lies in network effects. Most of the fast-growing marketing successes of our lifetime have spread because of ideas that work better when everyone knows them.

The early adopters have a huge incentive to bring your idea across the chasm to the masses; it will make their lives better if everyone in their network also uses this idea.

There's no reason to talk about a new kind of chocolate you really like. It doesn't make your life better if others eat it.

On the other hand, you spend a lot of time telling people about Snapchat or Instagram or Twitter, because if your friends followed you, your life would improve.

That's the simple ratchet power of network effects. *Connected tribes are more powerful than disconnected ones.* Individuals who get in early have an incentive to bring others along, and so they do.

It's not just technology, of course, although it is often the force behind the pattern interrupts that have remade our culture.

There's an incentive for me to organize a bus trip to

Washington, D.C., to protest gun violence. If more people come, not only will we make more of an impact, but the day will be more fun as well.

There's an incentive to get your friends to sign up for the local CSA farm share. The farmers can't afford to come for just a few people in the neighborhood, but if lots of people come, there will be better variety for all of us.

The peer-to-peer movement of ideas is how we cross the chasm—by giving people a network effect that makes the awkwardness of pitching change worth the effort.

The bridge is built on two simple questions:

1. What will I tell my friends?
2. Why will I tell them?

It is never the case that people will tell their friends because you want them to, or because you ask them to, or because you worked hard.

Give them a why. And that usually involves changing what you offer. Make things better by making better things—things that have a network effect, a ratchet, a reason for sharing.

Surviving the chasm

The Gartner Hype Cycle is a brilliant meta-analysis of how the culture changes.

The technology trigger opens the door for your art, for the contribution you want to make. It interrupts a pattern.

The Gartner Hype Cycle

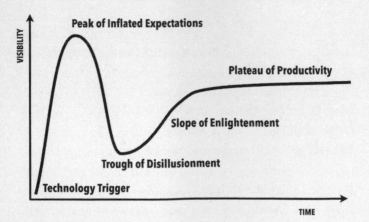

In that moment, marketing can help you reach the neophili-acs. Inevitably, these early adopters will hype your work. Of course they will. That's one of the best reasons to be an early adopter.

When the idea is presented to the rest of the market, it can't possibly compare to the hype. Hence the trough. This is another way to see Moore's chasm. It's in this moment, when the neo-philiacs are bored with you and the mass market disdains you, that you will most likely lose momentum. This is the moment when you need a bridge, a new way to step through the culture with stories that match the worldviews of this new, more con-servative market.

And then, with generous persistence, you can walk up the slope to the new plateau, the place where you are now indispensable to the masses. A new pattern replacing the old one.

You might not find the bridge

Years ago, my team at Squidoo launched hugdug.com.

The idea behind HugDug was pretty simple: You could build a page (it took about four minutes) profiling any product on Amazon that you loved. If you chose a book, for example, the page would bring in the cover, the title, and a big button with a link.

You'd add your own review and a bunch of relevant content.

If someone found the page and bought the book, Amazon would pay us a royalty, and we'd send half of it to your favorite charity. (This was years before smile.amazon.com, and we were donating twenty times as much to charity as they do.)

Our bet was that authors would happily promote their books in this way—it was easier to control than their Amazon page, and they could have pride in ownership in how the information was presented, not to mention the philanthropy of it all.

We also hoped that the typical Pinterest fan would find a page like this not only fun to build, but gratifying, because they'd be helping to raise money for a cause they cared about.

Our thesis was that we'd be able to put in the work to find the early adopters, neophiliacs eager to give shiny new things on the internet a try. We were betting that once they saw that it was working, they'd do it more, moving us deeper along the long tail, generating thousands of pages.

And that as the word spread, we'd bring in authors, and they'd be whales, promoting their books like crazy.

And that people who saw any of our HugDug pages would not only buy at the same rate they'd be buying on Amazon (after all, it was the same price), but would build their own pages (raising their status because they were sharing insights among an elite crowd, all in service of philanthropy).

We kept at it for months, but we failed.

I think the main reason we failed was that while we got trial (thousands of pages were built), we failed to find any whales. There were fewer than six people who built more than a dozen pages or promoted them very much.

The tension dissipated too quickly. People felt like they had no good reason to return after a single visit. The long tail was so long that it wasn't unusual for a HugDug page to sell zero books in a month. And most people were hesitant to promote a page, because even though it's easier now, it's still emotionally difficult to push your friends to visit a shopping site online.

The lesson was that a Kickstarter-like success is always more difficult than it looks. We were naïve in believing that four months was enough time to create an overnight success. We underestimated how difficult it might be to create sufficient incentives, and, most of all, we failed to create a tension dynamic that would have turned our early users into connected ambassadors who would have turned the ratchet as we crossed the chasm.

We didn't do enough to tell a story about status, and we weren't nearly specific enough about who our first customers would be, what they might have wanted, believed, and said.

Case Study: Facebook and crossing the biggest chasm

In our lifetime, very few brands have crossed over fully to the mass market. Starbucks, which is familiar to most people reading this, hasn't made it all the way, and neither has Heineken or even the bagel.

But Facebook has.

This graph shows what that looks like:

Each bar is users during a given year (the month changed midway, but the idea is the same). Sometime around 2008, a whole new bunch of everyone started using Facebook.

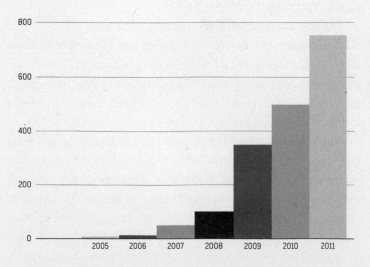

That leap happened because the reason for signing up changed from "this is sort of interesting" to "this will help me immeasurably" to "I'm the last person on earth who's not using this."

Starting at Harvard was part of the secret. The insecure Harvard student had an urgent status need: to find out where he or she stood in the pecking order.

As it spread through the Ivy League, Facebook crossed one local chasm after another. At each school, a neophiliac went first (because they like going first) but the relentless ratchet of status kept it spreading. The more friends you had on Facebook, the higher your status. The other people already on Facebook had a status you admired (other Ivy League students). Facebook was planted in the best possible spot, surrounded by insecure, high-status young people, with fast internet connections, plenty of spare time, and an insatiable desire to be seen, to connect, and to move up in some invisible hierarchy.

Once it spread through that local tribe, it wasn't hard to jump to other colleges, and then, finally, the public.

This last chasm leap is the billion-dollar one. And once again, status roles kick in. Because Facebook was able to combine nerdiness with status, they were able to surround the middle of the market and create an irresistible ratchet. Join in, or face your worst fear—be socially isolated.

As much as most marketers would like to make this last huge leap, it's unlikely. The market is just too big, and the typical network effect isn't that strong.

Crossing the local chasm

The good news is that you don't need to set out to cross a global chasm. A local one can change everything.

The local elementary school is a fine example. One kid brings in a yo-yo on Monday. But he's the wrong kid on the wrong day.

A few weeks later, a charismatic fifth-grader brings in her yo-yo, announcing that she's starting the Yo-yo Union, an exclusive club that's open to all. She's pretty good at tricks, but not so good that she's intimidating. And she brings three more yo-yos with her, for her friends.

Pretty soon, the four of them are out on the playground, walking dogs and sleeping. She's chosen wisely—each of these early adopters is a leader in her own right. A week later, there are thirty kids with yo-yos on the playground. The cost of entry is low, the payoff is quick, and the connection feels real.

A week later, it seems like the whole school is doing it.

Because yo-yos are a fad, without stickiness, they cool off as fast as they spread. Of course, it doesn't have to be that way if you build in identity and persistence.

The same crossing happened with Uggs, with black backpacks, with penny skateboards.

We only notice the ones that cross a local chasm, but the early adopters are always experimenting around the edges. It's when the combination of adoption and network effects creates enough tension for the idea to cross the local chasm that we notice it.

Clean water in a local village

For the lucky and privileged, clean water is a given. We've never known any other form of water.

For a billion people around the world, though, the norm is

dirty water, infested with parasites. Often requiring a walk of several hours to fetch, this water is essential for life, but it also makes people sick.

Consider the case of Water Health International. When WHI arrives in a village with its water purification kiosk, a few residents immediately understand the possibility for impact. They buy a special Jerry can from WHI and then pay to have it refilled every day. The few pennies spent on clean water are quickly earned back in time saved, increased productivity, and reduced medical expense.

And yet, not everyone buys the water right away. Most people don't. In fact, it follows precisely the same adoption curve as just about everything else, from toys to computers. The early adopters buy it first. They may be educated enough to realize how powerful an input clean water is, but it's more likely that they simply like buying things that are new.

Not only are these early adopters eager to go first, but they're eager to talk about their experience. The brightly colored water jugs that WHI requires (so they know that they're not refilling an infected vessel) are a badge of honor and an invitation to converse. But still, the early days are always fairly slow. Changing a multigenerational habit that's as close to survival as water is does not happen right away.

Still, the early adopters won't stop talking about it. It's not a fad; fresh water is needed daily, forever. And water is an easy thing to share and talk about.

To further the local shift, WHI sends representatives to the local school. Outfitted with a microscope projector, the rep works with the teacher and has each student bring in some water samples from their home.

Projecting the samples on the wall, the microscope tells a vivid story that resonates with the eight-year-olds in the class. This is what germs look like. This is what parasites look like. Inevitably, the students go home and tell their parents.

And now status kicks in.

When your young child talks about his neighbors having clean water . . . and you don't. When you see the respected members of the village hierarchy carrying the distinctive Jerry cans. When you hesitate to host someone in your home because you don't have clean water to offer them.

This is a ratchet, but not one based on obvious software network effects. It's based on the original network effect, the one built around people in proximity. As more and more people in the village get clean water, those without become socially isolated and feel stupid as well. Most can afford the water (because of the time and impact savings), but the emotional shift is the difficult part.

Within months, the water has crossed the local chasm from the early adopters to the rest of the village.

An aside about B2B marketing

B2B stands for business to business—when a business sells something to another one.

It's a third or more of many markets. And the marketing of B2B is no different.

It seems complicated, something completely separate. Huge numbers, RFPs, a focus on meeting spec, a price war, long sales cycles, and no fun at all.

But it's simpler than that.

Consider the growth of LEED certification in the United States. The Green Building Council has a set of efficiency standards that buildings (one of the most expensive items in the world) must meet. When they first launched, only two buildings a day were submitted for certification.

These were the early adopters—architects and builders who wanted something new to talk about.

At that rate, it would have taken a hundred years to hit the numbers they hit after just twelve.

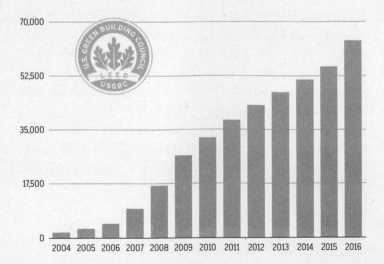

What happened? Just before the housing crisis hit, the number of certifications leapt forward, and it kept going. Why?

Think about it from the worldview of the real estate developer. He or she is about to spend a highly leveraged sum of money to build a building, a building for rent or eventual resale.

If just a few people insist on the LEED certification in a building they rent or buy, it's enough to confer status on people who have one of those buildings. And if you skimped when creating the building, you'd have to deal with the regret and fear you'd face if you ended up with a building seen by some as defective.

And so there's a race to the top.

Each developer has a narrative, and that narrative leads to the selfish (but ultimately positive) decision to get certified.

The one question that every business buyer asks herself is, "What will I tell my boss?"

You're marketing the answer to that question: "If you choose this, you can tell your board/investors/boss that you . . ."

The marketer who is out of ideas or energy finishes that sentence with, ". . . bought the cheapest one."

For the rest of us, there's the opportunity to finish that sentence with a narrative about status, fear, affiliation, belonging, dominion, safety, commitment, insight, or any of the other emotions we've discussed.

CHAPTER TWENTY

Organizing and Leading a Tribe

It's not your tribe

That's the first thing I say to people who talk about the folks they're lucky enough to work with and lead.

The tribe doesn't belong to you, so you don't get to tell the members what to do or to use them for your own aims.

If you're fortunate, there's a tribe that will listen to you and consider what you say.

If you're lucky, they'll interpret your words in a way that they believe will help them move the mission of the tribe forward, and you'll get a chance to do it again.

And if you invest in them, they'll show you what they want and what they need. You can gain empathy for them, understand their narrative, and serve them again.

The tribe would probably survive if you went away. The goal is for them to miss you if you did.

The power of now, not later

Marshall Ganz is the brilliant Harvard professor who has worked both with Cesar Chavez and Barack Obama. He has articulated a simple three-step narrative for action: the story of self, the story of us, and the story of now.

The story of self gives you standing, a platform from which to speak. When you talk about your transition—from who you used to be to who you became—you are being generous with us.

It's not about catastrophizing your situation or the faux empathy of online vulnerability. Instead, the story of self is *your chance to explain that you are people like us.* That you did things like this. That your actions led to a change, one we can hear and see and understand.

The story of us is the kernel of a tribe. Why are we alike? Why should we care? Can I find the empathy to imagine that I might be in your shoes?

The story of us is about together, not apart. It explains why your story of self is relevant to us, and how we will benefit when we're part of people like us.

And **the story of now** is the critical pivot. The story of now enlists the tribe on your journey. It's the peer opportunity/peer pressure of the tribe that will provide the tension for all of us to move forward, together.

I was like you. I was in the desert. Then I learned something and now I'm here.

Of course, I am not alone. I did not do this alone and I see in you the very pain I saw in myself. Together, we can make this better.

But if we hesitate, or if we leave the others behind, it won't work. The urgency of now requires that we do it together, without delay, without remorse, without giving in to our fear.

Story of self.

Story of us.

Story of now.

Here's a simple example: "I used to be fifty pounds overweight. My health was in tatters and my relationships were worse. Then I discovered competitive figure skating. It was tough at first, but thanks to my new friends on the rink, I got to the point where it was fun. Within months, I had lost dozens of pounds, but more important, I felt good about myself.

"The real win for me, though, was the friendships I made. I discovered that not only did I feel terrific physically, but being out on the ice with people—old friends like you, and the new ones I made at the rink—made me feel more alive.

"I'm so glad you were willing to come to the rink today. I called ahead and they've reserved some rental skates for you . . ."

In the first paragraph, we hear the story of our friend, a narrative of going from here to there.

In the second, we hear about how it changes our friend's relationships, including to people like us.

And in the third, there's a call to action, a reason to do something right now.

Manipulation is the tribe killer

In *Rules for Radicals*, noted labor organizer Saul Alinsky laid out thirteen principles that can be used in zero-sum game political settings to discourage and defeat enemies:

"Power is not only what you have but what the enemy thinks you have."

"Never go outside the expertise of your people."

"Whenever possible, go outside the expertise of the enemy."

"Make the enemy live up to its own book of rules."

"Ridicule is man's most potent weapon."

"A good tactic is one your people enjoy."

"A tactic that drags on too long becomes a drag."

"Keep the pressure on."

"The threat is usually more terrifying than the thing itself."

"The major premise for tactics is the development of operations that will maintain a constant pressure upon the opposition."

"If you push a negative hard and deep enough, it will break through into its counterside."

"The price of a successful attack is a constructive alternative."

"Pick the target, freeze it, personalize it, and polarize it."

Alas, this approach is now often used by both sides on just about any issue, and it tears away at civil discourse. When you're so sure you're right that you're willing to burn things down, it turns out that everyone is standing in a burning building sooner or later.

What happens if we reverse the rules?

"Put people to work. It's even more effective than money."

"Challenge your people to explore, to learn, and to get comfortable with uncertainty."

"Find ways to help others on the path find firm footing."

"Help others write rules that allow them to achieve their goals."

"Treat the others the way you'd want to be treated."

"Don't criticize for fun. Do it when it helps educate, even if it's not entertaining."

"Stick with your tactics long after everyone else is bored with them. Only stop when they stop working."

"It's okay to let the pressure cease now and then. People will pay attention to you and the change you seek when they are unable to consistently ignore it."

"Don't make threats. Do or don't do."

"Build a team with the capacity and the patience to do the work that needs doing."

"If you bring your positive ideas to the fore, again and again, you'll raise the bar for everyone else."

"Solve your own problems before you spend a lot of time finding problems for the others."

"Celebrate your people, free them to do even more, make it about the cohort, and invite everyone along. Disagree with institutions, not with people."

All thirteen of these principles get to the mission of the marketer. To engage with people and help them create the change they seek. To understand their worldviews and talk and act in ways that align with who they are and what they want. To connect people to one another in an infinite game of possibility.

Shared interests, shared goals, shared language

A tribe doesn't have to have a leader, but it often is populated with people who share interests, goals, and language.

Your opportunity as a marketer is the chance to connect the members of the tribe. They're lonely and disconnected, they fear being unseen, and you, as the agent of change, can make connection happen.

You can intentionally create cultural artifacts, to use status roles to elevate a costume, a series of code words, or even the secret handshake. You can be Betsy Ross and sew the flag (Betsy Ross herself, the very concept of Betsy Ross, is a symbol).

Don't say it all, and don't make it obvious. It's fine that there are secret handshakes, Easter eggs, and unknown features. It's fine that commitment and longevity earn an extra edge.

You can challenge the tribe to go further, encourage them to adopt goals, and push them forward. When Nike committed millions of dollars to Breaking2, a moonshot to break the two-hour mark on the marathon, they were engaging and challenging the tribe. Even if they don't succeed, they (and the tribe members who organize around them) will come out ahead.

Most of all, the tribe is waiting for you to commit.

They know that most marketers are fly-by-night operators, knocking on doors and moving on. But some, some hunker down and commit. And in return, the tribe commits to them.

Because once you're part of a tribe, your success is their success.

It will fade if you let it

There's the hope that you can spin up a movement and then get out of the way as it takes on a life of its own.

A vision that once you cross the local chasm, you'll become a permanent part of the culture and can move on to the next challenge.

In fact, that rarely happens.

There are always new ideas beckoning the early adopters. They're on the prowl, and they'll be the first to leave.

But those who admire the status quo might leave as well, once the tension is gone. They might have embraced your restaurant, your software, or your spiritual movement for a while, but the original status quo, the one they walked away from, persists as well, and without persistent and consistent inputs and new tension, they'll show up a bit less for you.

There's a half-life at work. For any tribal behavior that's not energetically maintained, half of the activity will disappear. Every day, every month, every year—it's not clear what the half-life for a given movement is, but you can expect that it will fade.

The alternative is to reinvest. To have the guts to sit with those you have instead of always being distracted to chase the next thing.

The best marketers are farmers, not hunters. Plant, tend, plow, fertilize, weed, repeat. Let someone else race around after shiny objects.

Take a room in town

Zig Ziglar was a door-to-door salesman of pots and pans. In the 1960s, this was a thing.

Most of the three thousand representatives in his company followed the same plan. They filled their cars with samples and hit the road. They'd visit a town, make all the easy sales, then get in the car and drive to the next town.

Early adopters, as we've seen, are easier to find and easier to sell to.

Zig had a different strategy.

He got in his car, found a new town, and moved in. He took a room for weeks at a time. He showed up and kept showing up.

Sure, he made the same early adopter sales as everyone else. But then people noticed he didn't leave like all the other salespeople that they'd seen before. He stayed.

By continuing to organize demonstration dinners, he got to know the people in town. He might engage with someone in the middle of the curve five or six or seven times over the course of a month.

Which is precisely what this sort of person wants before they make a decision.

Zig did the math. He understood that while most salespeople would flee when they hit the chasm, he could build a human bridge. There'd be days with no sales at all, but that's okay, because after crossing the local chasm, the volume would more than make up for the time invested.

The easy sales aren't always the important ones.

CHAPTER TWENTY-ONE

Some Case Studies Using the Method

"How do I get an agent?"

That's the question that screenwriters, directors, and actors get asked all the time. The industry has gatekeepers, and you don't have the keys to the gate, so an agent is the answer.

As Brian Koppelman has generously pointed out, it doesn't work in this direct a manner. Sure, the agent will field calls for you, but he's not going to become your full-time sales rep, making calls night and day and tirelessly promoting you to the industry.

The method isn't to go out and find an agent. The method is to do work so impossibly magical that agents and producers come looking for you.

You, the one who cared enough to put it all on the table, who fell in love with your viewers and your craft, and who made something that mattered.

It doesn't have to be a feature film or a Pulitzer-winning play. In fact, the approach works best if it's not a fully polished and complete creation.

The best work will create an imbalance in the viewer, one that can only be remedied by spreading the word, by experiencing this with someone else. The tension this imbalance creates forces the word to spread. It means that asking, "Have you seen . . . ?" raises the status of the asker, and the champions multiply.

What matters is the connection you made. Everyone has ten friends, fifty colleagues, a hundred acquaintances. And you can cajole them into seeing your work . . . and then what happens?

If it's electric, if it makes an impact, if the right sort of tension is created, they'll have to tell someone else.

Because telling someone else is what humans do. It's particularly what we do if we work with ideas. Telling others about how we've changed is the only way to relieve our tension.

This is the hard work we discovered many pages ago. The hard work of deciding that this is your calling, of showing up for those you seek to change.

Do that first.

Tesla broke the other cars first

When the Tesla Model S was launched, its primary function was to tell a story that, for a lot of luxury car neophiliacs, would break their current car.

Break it in the sense that it wasn't fun to own anymore.

Wasn't worth bragging about.

Didn't increase their status as a smart, wealthy person, who was clearly smarter and wealthier than everyone else.

This luxury car owner went to sleep the night before, delighted that the car in the garage was shiny, new, and state of the art. That it was safe, efficient, and worthy.

And then he or she woke up to discover that the story was no longer true.

Tesla understood that no one who bought one of the first fifty thousand Teslas actually needed a car. They all had perfectly fine cars.

So Elon Musk created a car that changed the story that a specific group told themselves, a story that undid their status as early adopters and as tech geeks and as environmentalists and as those that supported audacity.

All at once.

The existing car companies have always had a hard time turning concept cars into real ones. They launch concept cars at auto shows to normalize them, to socialize the innovations, to make it more likely that the real car, years down the road, won't bomb.

They couldn't launch the Tesla. Not because they didn't know how (they did) and not because they didn't have the resources (they did). No, Ford and GM and Toyota didn't launch the Tesla because car companies like us don't take risks like this. And their customers felt the same way.

Making a car that could have the impact the Tesla did on the story of luxury cars wasn't easy. Musk chose to go to difficult extremes in positioning the car on behalf of his fans: it's the fastest, the safest, and the most efficient car of its size, ever. All three.

This audacity is available to more and more organizations as technology shifts from "Could it be done?" to "Do we have the guts?"

The NRA as a role model

There are few groups more controversial than the National Rifle Association. But as focused nonprofit/political marketers, they have no peer.

They have only five million members, less than 2 percent of the population, but have used that base to change the attitude and focus of thousands of lawmakers. They are regularly vilified by the masses but continue to confound expectations in their impact, revenue, and profile.

When nonprofits talk about changing hearts and minds, when they target "everyone" and seek to get bigger, they can learn critical strategic lessons from the NRA instead. By focusing on the minimal viable audience (just five million people), the NRA is very comfortable saying, "It's not for you."

By activating those members and making it easy for them to talk to their friends, they're able to create significant leverage. A Pew study shows that gun owners are more than twice as likely to contact government officials about their issues than nonowners are.

The NRA intentionally creates "people like us." They're comfortable with insiders and outsiders, and often issue public statements that are, at their best, viciously divisive. They have bent a corner of the culture in significant ways, and they've done it not by changing worldviews but by embracing them.

The NRA isn't my version of "better," but it clearly resonates with those that they seek to serve.

This persistent, disciplined approach to an issue is precisely how much of the change has been made in our culture.

Getting the boss to say yes

It's one thing to market to the world, but it feels quite different to market to one person . . . like your boss.

Except it's not. Not really.

Your boss is probably not eager to change her worldview. She wants what she's always wanted. She sees things through the lens of her experience, not yours. She is aware of who the people like us are, and what they think. She wants to do things that help her achieve her goals, which probably include status, safety, and respect.

If you go to her with what you want, with a focus on price or features or false urgency, it's unlikely to lead to the answer you seek.

If you go to her asking for authority without offering responsibility, that too is unlikely to get you very far.

But if you can dig deep and see the status roles, can decode dominion versus affiliation, and can use trust to earn enrollment, the process can change.

You can produce better by serving the people you market to. Turning them from customers to students. Gaining enrollment. Teaching. Connecting. Step by step, drip by drip.

CHAPTER TWENTY-TWO

Marketing Works, and Now It's Your Turn

The tyranny of perfect

Perfect closes the door. It asserts that we're done, that this is the best we can do.

Worse, perfect forbids us to try. To seek perfection and not reach it is a failure.

The possibility of better

Better opens the door. Better challenges us to see what's there and begs us to imagine how we could improve on that.

Better invites us in and gives us a chance to seek dramatic improvement on behalf of those we seek to serve.

The magic of good enough

Good enough isn't an excuse or a shortcut. Good enough leads to engagement.

Engagement leads to trust.

Trust gives us a chance to see (if we choose to look).

And seeing allows us to learn.

Learning allows us to make a promise.

And a promise might earn enrollment.

And enrollment is precisely what we need to achieve better.

Ship your work. It's good enough.

Then make it better.

Help!

When we offer it, we're being generous.

When we ask for it, we're trusting someone else to see us and care about us.

On the other hand, when someone refuses to offer help or ask for it, everyone is closed, on defense, afraid of the other.

If there's no connection, we can't make things better.

CHAPTER TWENTY-THREE

Marketing to the Most Important Person

Is marketing evil?

If you spend time and money (with skill) you can tell a story that spreads, that influences people, that changes actions. Marketing can cause people to buy something that they wouldn't have bought without marketing, vote for someone they might not have considered, and support an organization that would have been invisible otherwise.

If marketing doesn't work, then a lot of us are wasting a great deal of effort (and cash). But it does.

So, does that make marketing evil? In a story about my blog published in *Time* magazine, the author wrote, tongue in cheek, "Entry you'll never see: Is marketing evil? Based on a long career in the business, I'd have to answer 'yes.'"

Actually, I need to amend what this pundit said. I'll add this entry: Are marketers evil? Based on a long career in the business, I'd have to answer, "Some of them."

I think it's evil to persuade kids to start smoking, to cynically manipulate the electoral or political process, to lie to people in ways that cause disastrous side effects. I think it's evil to sell an ineffective potion when an effective medicine is available. I think it's evil to come up with new ways to make smoking acceptable so you can make a few more bucks.

Marketing is beautiful when it persuades people to get a polio vaccine or to wash their hands before performing surgery. Marketing is powerful when it sells a product to someone who discovers more joy or more productivity because he bought it. Marketing is magic when it elects someone who changes the community for the better. Ever since Josiah Wedgwood invented marketing a few centuries ago, it has been used to increase productivity and wealth.

I've got a lot of nerve telling you that what you do might be immoral. It's immoral to rob someone's house and burn it to the ground, but is it immoral to market them into foreclosure? Well, if marketing works, if it's worth the time and money we spend on it, then I don't think it matters a bit if you're "just doing your job." It's still wrong.

Just like every powerful tool, the impact comes from the craftsman, not the tool. Marketing has more reach, with more speed, than it has ever had before. With less money, you can have more impact than anyone could have imagined just ten years ago. The question, one I hope you'll ask yourself, is *What are you going to do with that impact?*

For me, marketing works for society when the marketer and consumer are both aware of what's happening and are both satisfied with the ultimate outcome. I don't think it's evil to make someone happy by selling them cosmetics, because beauty isn't the goal—it's the process that brings joy. On the other hand, swindling someone out of their house in order to make a sales commission . . .

Just because you can market something doesn't mean you should. You've got the power, so you're responsible, regardless of what your boss tells you to do.

The good news is that I'm not in charge of what's evil and what's not. You, your customers, and their neighbors are. The even better news is that ethical, public marketing will eventually defeat the kind that depends on the shadows.

What will you build now?

What do we do about the noise in our heads?

Where do we find the strength to bring our *better* to the world?

Why is it so hard to develop a point of view? Why do we hesitate when we say to the world, "Here, I made this"? And what's the alternative to hesitating?

These don't sound like marketing questions, but in fact, if you let them sit unanswered, they're getting in the way of your marketing. People who aren't as gifted or generous as you are running circles around you, because they are showing up as professionals. And yet, too many people with something to offer are holding themselves back.

There's a difference between being good at what you do, being good at making a thing, and being good at marketing. We need your craft, without a doubt. But we need your change even more.

It's a leap to choose to make change. It feels risky, fraught with responsibility. And it might not work.

If you bring your best self to the world, your best work, and the world doesn't receive it, it's entirely possible that your marketing sucked.

It's entirely possible that you have empathy for what people were feeling.

It's entirely possible that you chose the wrong axes, and that you failed to go to the edges.

It's entirely possible you were telling the wrong story to the wrong person in the wrong way on the right day, or even on the wrong day.

Fine, but that's not about you.

That's about your work as a marketer.

And you can get better at that craft.

This thing that we do—whether it's surgery or gardening or marketing—it's not *us*, it's the work that we do.

We're humans. Our work isn't us. As humans, we can choose to do the work, and we can choose to improve our work.

If we're going to take it personally every time someone doesn't click on a link, every time someone doesn't renew, we can't possibly do our work as professionals. And thus we get stuck in search of perfect. Stuck without empathy. Stuck in a corner, bleeding and in pain, because we've been personally maligned.

One way to avoid that is to realize that marketing is a process and a craft.

Just because the pot you made on the wheel broke in the kiln doesn't mean you're not a good person. It simply means your pot broke and that maybe some lessons in pottery will help you go forward. You're capable of doing better.

Realize that as a marketer, the *better* you are trying to teach or sell to the right person is worth far more than what you are charging.

If you are seeking to raise money for a charity, someone who donates a hundred or a thousand or a million dollars is only going to do it if they get more value than it costs them to donate. If you're selling a widget for a thousand dollars, the only people who buy it will buy it because they believe it's worth more than a thousand dollars.

We bring value to the world when we market. That's why people engage with us.

If you don't market the change you'd like to contribute, then you're stealing.

Here you are offering more value than you're charging. It's a bargain. A gift.

If you hesitate to market your offering properly, it's not that you're being shy. It's not that you're being circumspect. It's that you're stealing, because there's someone who needs to learn from you, engage with you, or buy from you.

Someone will benefit from your better if you get out of your way and market it.

There's a student who's ready to sign up. There's somebody who wants a guide, who wants to go somewhere. If you hesitate to extend yourself with empathy, to hear them, you're letting us down.

The marketer's contribution is willingness to see and be seen.

To do that, we need to be able to market to ourselves, to sell ourselves every day. To sell ourselves on the difference we're able to make, if we persist with generosity and care.

You're already telling yourself a story. Every day.

We may market to ourselves that we are struggling. We may tell ourselves that we are unknown and deserve to be unknown. We may tell ourselves that we're a fake, a fraud, a manipulator. We may tell ourselves that we are unjustly ignored.

They're as true as we want them to be. And if you tell yourself a story enough times, you will make it true.

Make things better. It's entirely possible that the thing you are marketing satisfies no real demand, there is no good strategy behind it, and that you are being selfish in thinking that just because you built it you should stick with it.

Blow it up. Start over. Make something you're proud of. Market something you're proud of. But once you've done that, once you've looked someone in the eye and they have asked, "Will you do that again for me?," once you have brought value to a student because you taught them and helped them get to the next step, do it again, and then do it again. Because we need your contribution. And if you're having trouble making your contribution, realize your challenge is a story you are marketing to yourself.

It is the marketing we do for ourselves, to ourselves, by ourselves, the story we tell ourselves, that can change everything. It's what's going to enable you to create value, to be missed if you were gone.

I can't wait to see what you build next.

A Marketing Reading List
(in no particular order)

There are a thousand books I'd love for you to read, but I've tried to highlight books that are primarily focused around marketing, particularly around the kind of marketing we've been discussing in this book.

Crossing the Chasm by Geoff Moore

The Long Tail: Why the Future of Business Is Selling Less of More by Chris Anderson

My Life in Advertising and *Scientific Advertising* by Claude Hopkins

Ogilvy on Advertising by David Ogilvy

Adcreep by Mark Bartholomew

Who Do You Want Your Customers to Become? (A short modern classic by Michael Schrage.)

Creating Customer Evangelists: How Loyal Customers Become a Volunteer Salesforce by Jackie Huba and Ben McConnell

The New Rules of Marketing and PR: How to Use Social Media, Online Video, Mobile Applications, Blogs, News Releases, and Viral Marketing to Reach Buyers Directly by David Meerman Scott

Secrets of Closing the Sale (Zig Ziglar's book is as much about marketing as sales.)

Positioning: The Battle for Your Mind by Jack Trout and Al Ries

Purple Cow: Transform Your Business by Being Remarkable by Seth Godin

Tribes: We Need You to Lead Us by Seth Godin

All Marketers are Liars by Seth Godin (Of all my marketing-related books, this is the one that's the most on point.)

Unleashing the Ideavirus: Stop Marketing AT People! Turn Your Ideas into Epidemics by Helping Your Customers Do the Marketing for You (One more from me.)

Direct Mail Copy That Sells by Herschell Gordon Lewis (One of his many classic books on copywriting.)

A New Brand World: Eight Principles for Achieving Brand Leadership in the Twenty-First Century by Scott Bedbury and Stephen Fenichell

The Culting of Brands: Turn Your Customers into True Believers by Douglas Atkin (An overlooked gem.)

Selling the Dream by Guy Kawasaki (His best book.)

The Four Steps to the Epiphany by Steve Blank (A startup book with essential marketing insight.)

The Tipping Point: How Little Things Can Make a Big Difference by Malcolm Gladwell

Marketing: A Love Story: How to Matter to Your Customers (Bernadette Jiwa is brilliant and I recommend all her books.)

Syrup by Max Barry (The best marketing novel ever written.)

Free: The Future of a Radical Price by Chris Anderson

Rocket Surgery Made Easy by Steve Krug (A surprising book about testing.)

The Guerrilla Marketing Handbook by Jay Levinson and Seth Godin

The Regis Touch by Regis McKenna

New Rules for the New Economy by Kevin Kelly

Talking to Humans: Success Starts with Understanding Your Customers by Giff Constable (An extended blog post about talking to customers.)

The Tom Peters Seminar: Crazy Times Call for Crazy Organizations by Tom Peters

The Pursuit of Wow! Every Person's Guide to Topsy-Turvy Times by Tom Peters

Start with Why by Simon Sinek

The Experience Economy, Updated Edition by Joseph Pine and James Gilmore

Meaningful Work by Shawn Askinosie

The Ultimate Question 2.0: How Net Promoter Companies Thrive in a Customer-Driven World by Fred Reichheld

Business Model Generation (On How to Build a Business That Matches the Marketing You Want to Do) by Alexander Osterwalder and Yves Pigneur

The War of Art and *Do the Work* by Steve Pressfield (On why you might be having a hard time doing what you know will work.)

A Simple Marketing Worksheet

- Who's it for?
- What's it for?
- What is the worldview of the audience you're seeking to reach?
- What are they afraid of?
- What story will you tell? Is it true?
- What change are you seeking to make?
- How will it change their status?
- How will you reach the early adopters and neophiliacs?
- Why will they tell their friends?
- What will they tell their friends?
- Where's the network effect that will propel this forward?
- What asset are you building?
- Are you proud of it?

ACKNOWLEDGMENTS

. . . . .

All I can do is borrow. I don't know of any purely original ideas, ones that arrive from the sky on a bolt of lightning. And if I borrow great ideas and recombine them in interesting ways, perhaps I can contribute something to the next person.

In this book, I've done even more borrowing than usual. From Michael Schrage for the germ of the change idea, from Bernadette Jiwa who has done such generous work on stories, and from Tom Peters, well, about everything. There are a few riffs included from my blog, which is published daily. And of course, thanks to Pam Slim, Jackie Huba, Jenny Blake, Brian Koppelman, Michael Bungay Stanier, Alex Peck, Steve Pressfield, Shawn Coyne, Al Pittampalli, Ishita Gupta, Clay Hebert, Alex DiPalma, David Meerman Scott (Deadhead), Amy Koppelman, Nicole Walters, Brené Brown, Marie Forleo, WillieJackson.com, Jacqueline Novogratz, John Wood, Scott Harrison, Cat Hoke, Michael Tremonte, Keller Williams, Tim Ferriss, Patricia Barber, Harley Finkelstein, Fiona McKean, Lil Zig Ballesteros, Zig Ziglar, David Ogilvy, Jay Levinson, Sheryl Sandberg, Adam Grant, Susan Piver, Aria Finger, Nancy Lublin, Chris Fralic, Kevin Kelly, Lisa Gansky, Roz Zander, Ben

Zander, Micah Sifry, Micah Solomon, Teri Tobias, Tina Roth Eisenberg, Paul Jun, Jack Trout, Al Ries, John Acker, Rohan Rajiv, Niki Papadopoulos, Vivian Roberson, the generous students at The MarketingSeminar.com, and coaches Travis Wilson, Françoise Hontoy, Scott Perry, Louise Karch, as well as the extraordinary Kelli Wood, Marie Schacht, Sam Miller, and Fraser Larock. And Maya P. Lim, Jenn Patel, and Lisa DiMona..Thanks to Alex, Sarah, Leo, and Future Peck, as well as the alumni and coaches of altmba.com.

Always and endless special thanks to Alex Godin, Mo Godin, and of course, Helene.

Code: seven5six6

INDEX

ABOUT THE AUTHOR

· · · · ·

In 2018, Seth Godin was inducted into the AMA Marketing Hall of Fame. That's the culmination of more than thirty years of teaching, leading, starting, collaborating, failing, engaging, and seeking.

Seth runs TheMarketingSeminar.com, which is the intensive workshop that this book is based on. He also created the altMBA, a remarkable monthlong workshop that helps leaders level up. Seth is the author of eighteen best-sellers that have been translated into more than thirty-five languages, and the writer of one of the most popular blogs in the world, found at seths.blog.

He's worked with Jay Levinson, Bernadette Jiwa, Adrian Zackheim, Lester Wunderman, TED, Jay Chiat, Tom Peters, Michelle Kydd Lee, Jerry Shereshewsky, the *Harvard Business Review*, NYU, the MIT Media Lab, Mayor Alan Webber, Bill Taylor, Steve Wozniak, Steve Pressfield, Krista Tippett, Cat Hoke, Scott Harrison, Michelle Welsch, Jacqueline Novogratz, and change-makers, leaders, and makers of ruckuses around the world. Find out more at TheMarketingSeminar.com

More from Seth Godin

What to Do When It's Your Turn

The Icarus Deception

V is for Vulnerable

altMBA.com

TheMarketingSeminar.com

Linchpin

Tribes

The Dip

Free Prize Inside

Purple Cow

FIND THEM ALL AT SETHGODIN.COM